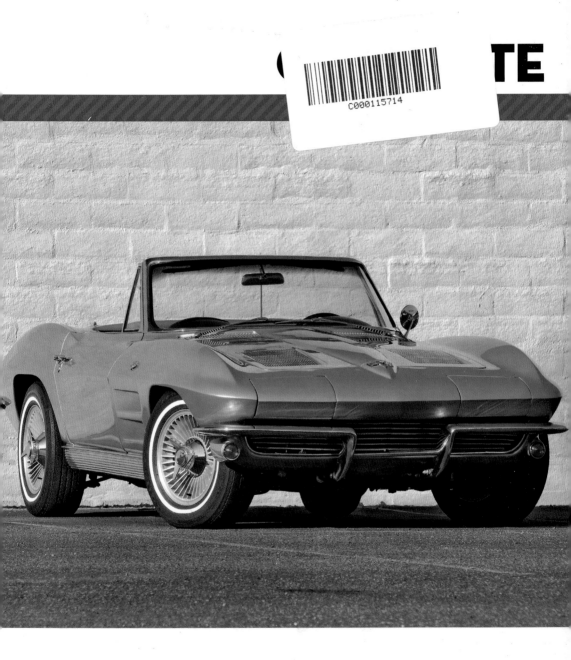

First published in 2012 by Motorbooks, an imprint of MBI Publishing Company, 400 First Avenue North, Suite 300, Minneapolis, MN 55401 USA

Motorbooks titles are also available at discounts in bulk quantity for industrial or promotional use. For details write to Special Sales Manager at MBI Publishing Company, 400 First Avenue North, Suite 300, Minneapolis, MN 55401 USA.

To find out more about our books, visit us online at www.motorbooks.com.

Library of Congress Cataloging-in-Publication Data

Newhardt, David, 1955-
  Corvette / David Newhardt.
    p. cm. -- (First gear)
  ISBN 978-0-7603-4223-7 (pbk.)
  1. Corvette automobile--Pictorial works. 2. Corvette automobile--History--Chronology. I. Title.
  TL215.C6N475 2012
  629.222'2--dc23
                              2012008466

On the front cover: 2011 Corvette ZR1
On the back cover: (top to bottom) Harley Earl's 1963 Corvette Roadster, 1990 Corvette ZR-1, and 2009 Corvette Coupe
On the title page: 1963 Corvette Sting Ray Roadster
P230-31: main: Ferenc Szelepcsenyi/Shutterstock.com: **inset:** Daniel Goodings/Shutterstock.com
P232: top: Balazs Toth/Shutterstock.som; **bottom:** Ferenc Szelepcsenyi/Shutterstock.com
P233: top: Neil Balderson/Shutterstock.com; **bottom:** Oskar Schuler/Shutterstock.com

Editor: Scott Pearson and Jeffrey Zuehlke
Design Manager: Brad Springer
Series design: Laura Rades

CONTENTS

ACKNOWLEDGMENTS

This book was a labor of love. I got my start as an automotive journalist many years ago, writing and shooting for *Vette Vues Magazine*. Over the years, I've had my work in many other periodicals, and I'm currently on the masthead of *Corvette Magazine*. So when editor Jeffrey Zuehlke asked if I'd like to create a book introducing people to the wonderful world of the Corvette, I couldn't sign the contract fast enough.

I speak about Corvettes from experience: my daily driver for eight years was a 1966 coupe. Both my newborn sons came home from the hospital under its huge rear window. It was with a heavy heart that I sold it to buy a more family-friendly vehicle. But over the years, I've been fortunate to slip behind the wheel of many Corvettes, and their magic continues to fascinate me.

It's impossible to create a book without help, especially a tome about automobiles. Without the assistance of many people, I'd still be staring at a blank computer screen and my cameras would stay in their bags. Here, in no particular order, are the people and organizations that have helped me celebrate America's original sports car: Chevrolet Motor Division, Bernie DeMarkey, Dana Mecum, Sam Murtaugh, Dan McMichael, the Corvette Owners Club of San Diego, Jim Parkinson, Harry Rieger, Kenn Funk, Michael Smyth, Brad Kleinman, Page One Automotive, Randy Leffingwell, Jim Mangione, Eric Gustafson, Jay Leno, Helga Pollock, Reeves Callaway, Ron Austin, Michael McCafferty, Fred and Deni Fossek, Randy Standke, Sharon Sceper, "Corvette Mike" Vietro, Joel Rosen, Martyn L. Schorr, Bernard Juchli, Bob Sales, Darwin Holmstrom, and Zack Miller.

Thank you.
David Newhardt,
Pasadena, California

INTRODUCTION

Thank the British for the Corvette. Really. Without the spindly, low-slung, wire-wheeled affairs that American servicemen took a shine to while stationed in England in the late 1940s, the Corvette never would have happened. After World War II, the American automobile industry took up where it had left off in December 1941, making full-size, heavy vehicles that were ideal for taking the family on a cross-country journey but lacked anything resembling fun. On the other side of the Pond, the Brits were used to making smaller, more nimble cars, such as MGs and Jaguars, in part because the roads were narrower but also because a smaller car requires less material. Upon the cessation of hostilities in 1945, raw materials were in very short supply in the UK. People wanted their own transportation, but with a finite amount of metal, British carmakers built what they knew best, vehicles of diminutive stature.

American servicemen in the British Isles drove the local cars and loved the way they hugged the road and created fun wherever they went. Many servicemen brought their

English cars home to America with them, and soon they were buzzing around from Mulholland Drive to Wall Street. It didn't take long for American racetracks to be filled with the sound of angry English sports cars, and in Detroit people took notice. Granted, the quantity of imported sports cars in America was tiny, but they had an influence beyond their numbers.

Harley Earl, the head of General Motors' Art and Colour Section, the in-house design department, loved the idea of a small, sporty vehicle in the GM lineup; it would represent the youth and optimism that he wanted GM products to exude. But with America embroiled in the Korean War, valuable materials such as steel were in short supply. So he had his studios create a visually exciting two-seat concept car, built out of fiberglass, a material new to the automobile industry. Fiberglass made it easy to create compound curves, and it was rustproof and lightweight as well. The intention was to make a concept car out of fiberglass, then switch to steel for the body of the production vehicles.

Using a modified production Chevrolet frame and a 150-horsepower straight-six engine called the Blue Flame Special to save costs, Earl unveiled his creation at the 1953 Motorama show, a traveling event that gave the public in six cities a chance to see possible future designs. The response to the Polo White–painted car was enthusiastic, and the decision to put the vehicle into production was soon made. General Motors wanted to strike fast, getting the new car on the street as soon as possible. But a steel body would take too long develop, so GM decided to stick with fiberglass. And in a discreet nod to the roots of the vehicle, a photographer named Myron Scott, who worked for the Campbell Ewald advertising agency, came up with the name of a small, nimble British warship: *Corvette*. So overwhelming was the public's response to the Chevrolet Corvette that Ford rushed the 1955 Thunderbird, its own two-seater, to market.

Since its introduction, the Corvette has been an aspirational vehicle and, in the hands of Zora Arkus-Duntov and his engineers, an effective race car. It's been a star on road courses, drag strips, and movie screens. It has been owner modified for decades, and it has created one of the finest single-marque automotive organizations, the National Corvette Restorers Society. A thriving aftermarket industry has grown around the needs of Corvette owners, and the Chevrolet two-seater continues to attract more fans every year. It has been the Chevrolet flagship since 1953, and with the imminent release of the sixth-generation Corvette, it's clear that this American icon isn't going anywhere except down the road, quickly.

CHAPTER 1
FIRST GENERATION, 1953-1962

With the overwhelming demand for the new Corvette following the GM Motorama show at New York City's Waldorf Astoria Hotel in January 1953, Chevrolet had to get some cars into the public's hands, and pronto. A temporary facility was pressed into duty in Flint, Michigan, to build 300 1953 Corvettes. Due to the scarcity of the car, General Motors felt that getting the car into the hands of high-profile individuals, such as movie stars and professional athletes, would increase the exposure of the new sports car.

Production for model year 1954 moved to St. Louis, Missouri, where the Corvettes would be built until 1981. Still available with just a six-cylinder engine, the Corvette, while well received, didn't sell in the expected numbers. The introduction of a V-8 engine for 1955 didn't exactly spark a stampede into dealerships, and General Motors thought about pulling the plug on the car.

But a GM engineer, Zora Arkus-Duntov, saw the potential within the Corvette. He pushed for changes that transformed the Corvette from boulevard cruiser to genuine sports car. A new body for 1956 gave the car a sleeker, more purposeful look, and a score of Duntov-driven changes under the skin created a true sports car.

The introduction of mechanical fuel injection for 1957 raised the performance level of the Corvette to a point where it could genuinely compete with European sports cars. As the 1950s came to a close, American automobile designers' fascination with the "bigger is better" philosophy even extended to the Corvette. The body gained heft, the option list grew longer, and the engines became more powerful. While this wasn't everyone's cup of tea, no one could deny that the Corvette was truly America's sports car.

Under its voluptuous fiberglass body, the new Corvette borrowed much from the staid Chevrolet sedans of 1953. With a beefy chassis incorporating an X-brace and a straight-six engine bolted to a two-speed Powerglide automatic transmission, the Corvette was anything but fragile. Actually, it was a bit slow compared with its intended competition, the Jaguar XK-120. And the Corvette cost $268 more than the Jaguar. Each 1953 Corvette was essentially a

1953 CORVETTE ROADSTER

Price: $3,498
Engine: 150-horsepower, 235-cubic-inch, inline six
0–60: 11.0 seconds
Top speed: 105 miles per hour

hand-built automobile, as the alignment of each fiberglass panel had to be adjusted on the assembly line. Plastic slide-in side windows didn't do much to convey a

high-end aura, and neither did a leaking convertible top. Yet the press was impressed and gave the Corvette a hearty welcome. Every 1953 Corvette was finished in Polo White paint, with a Sportsman Red interior.

The first Corvette rolled off the assembly line on Van Slyke Road in Flint, Michigan, on June 30, 1953. Two were built that day, and it's suspected that they were test-driven to destruction. Corvette serial number E53F001003 has survived and is in the hands of a collector. Production at the Flint facility ended on December 24, 1953, and on December 28, 1953, the assembly line for the 1954 Corvettes started. But the '53 Corvette was the first series production automobile with a fiberglass body.

Did You Know?

When the first production Corvette, serial number E53F001001, rolled off the assembly line, worker Tony Klieber was behind the wheel.

By the third year of production, the initial demand for the car had been satisfied, and sales had taken a precipitous drop. When the 1955 Corvette went on sale, more than 1,100 1954 models were still sitting on dealer lots. Something had to be done, so Chevrolet slipped its new 265-cubic-inch V-8 engine into most of the 700 cars built for 1955; a handful rolled off the assembly line with the Blue Flame straight-six. Color choices expanded, and for the first time, a three-speed manual transmission was available. A modest list of options wasn't really optional; virtually every 1955 Corvette had all the options installed.

But Chevy had serious egg on its face with the release of the new Ford Thunderbird the same year. A two-seat personal car, it was well built, powered by a 292-cubic-inch V-8, and dramatically

styled. Ford sold 16,000 for 1955. Chevrolet realized that it had better do something radical with the Corvette or the Thunderbird would turn the fiberglass vehicle into a mere footnote. Fortunately, the Corvette had powerful friends within General Motors. They decided to pull the car away from the personal car mold and take it into uncharted territory: creating a true sports car.

1955 CORVETTE ROADSTER

Price: $2,909 (V-8)
Engine: 195-horsepower, 265-cubic-inch V-8
0–60: 8.7 seconds
Top speed: 119 miles per hour

Did You Know?

Six-cylinder Corvettes used a 6-volt electrical system, while V-8s utilized a 12-volt system.

In the handful of years since the Corvette had debuted, its purpose, thanks to Zora Arkus-Duntov, had settled firmly on competition. Duntov, a former racer and now the Corvette's chief engineer, was a forward-thinking force of nature who lived by the creed, "If power is good, more power is better." When General Motors moved to put a mechanical fuel-injection system onto production vehicles, Duntov was at the front of the line, insisting that the flagship of Chevrolet be offered with it.

1957 CORVETTE ROADSTER, FUEL INJECTED

Price: $3,902
Engine: 283-horsepower, 283-cubic-inch V-8
0–60: 5.7 seconds
Top speed: 134 miles per hour

Four levels of "Ramjet" fuel-injected fun were available, ranging from 250 to 283 horsepower. Tipping the scales at just 2,849 pounds, the Corvette responded as few street cars ever had. It wasn't an accident

that racing grids were soon full of Corvettes, trouncing virtually everything else on the track. Only 1,040 Corvettes were equipped with fuel injection in 1957. This was also the first year that a four-speed manual transmission was available in the Corvette. Who says racing doesn't improve the breed?

With its dual headlights and clean lines, the 1957 Corvette sold well, almost doubling in sales from the year before. A total of 6,339 Corvettes went to good homes for 1957.

Did You Know?

Equipment that's standard on today's Corvette was optional in 1957. This included windshield washers, a heater, power windows, and an AM radio.

When Texas meets Italy, there's no telling what will happen. In 1959 a trio of Texans—Gary Laughlin, Jim Hall, and Carroll Shelby—wanted to put a strong American engine into a sports car cloaked in swoopy European bodywork. Laughlin's Ferrari Monza's crankshaft had broken, and he was fed up with fragile European machinery. The trio sent three 1959 Corvette chassis and engines to Italian design firm Carrozzeria

1959 CORVETTE SCAGLIETTI

Price: $9,200
Engine: 315-horsepower, 283-cubic-inch V-8
0–60: 8.1 seconds
Top speed: 133 miles per hour

Scaglietti with instructions to clothe the burly American components in aluminum panels. The Texans hoped to interest

Chevrolet in providing running chassis, and a bespoke coachbuilder would provide the bodies. They would reap the rewards.

Scaglietti's biggest client was Ferrari, and after almost two years of work, the three resulting Corvette Scagliettis closely resembled a trio of Ferraris. Of course, with their thumping, fuel-injected V-8s, they didn't sound like any Ferrari. But Enzo Ferrari was not pleased. He told Scaglietti that if it continued to build these vehicles for the Americans, there wouldn't be any more business from Maranello. End of program.

After that, Chevrolet declined to provide any further chassis, so Shelby took his idea to Ford Motor Company. The result was the Cobra.

Did You Know?
By replacing the stock fiberglass body with hand-formed aluminum, the finished car was 400 pounds lighter than a regular Corvette.

The Corvette entered the "swingin' sixties" as a refinement of the previous year's offering. Under the curvaceous fiberglass were new front and rear anti-sway bars, which helped control body lean under heavy cornering. By making the clutch housing out of aluminum, the designers shaved 18 pounds from the curb weight. With a menu of 283-cubic-inch powerplants kicking out horsepower ranging from 230 to 290,

1960 CORVETTE ROADSTER

Price: $3,872
Engine (base): 230-horsepower, 283-cubic-inch V-8
0–60: 8.4 seconds
Top speed: 124 miles per hour

and with both automatic and manual transmissions offered, a Corvette could be tailored to suit any customer, from weekday commuter to weekend racer.

Sales for the 1960 Corvette were 10,261 units, an improvement from 1959's 9,670 cars sold. The Corvette was now firmly lodged in the public's mind as a true sports car. No stranger to racetracks or the checkered flag, the Corvette was the flagship in the Chevrolet line; period advertisements boasted of its prowess on the track. This was the era of "win on Sunday, sell on Monday," and Chevrolet used the Corvette to full advantage in drawing customers into showrooms. While not every "up" who walked into the dealership would drive away in the two-seat sports car, the odds were good that a new Bowtie product would be in the garage that night.

Did You Know?

The TV show *Route 66* featured Martin Milner and George Maharis saving the day each week behind the wheel of a 1960 Corvette.

The most obvious external change to the Corvette for 1962 was the elimination of the chrome trim around the side cove. Contrasting colors in the cove were no longer an option. But to make up for that loss was a bigger engine under the hood: 327 cubic inches. Both bore and stroke were increased, and the enlarged displacement allowed the base engine's 10.5:1 compression to deliver 250 ponies. Buyers with deeper pockets could shell out

1962 CORVETTE ROADSTER

Price: $4,038
Engine (base): 250-horsepower, 327-cubic-inch V-8
0–60: 5.9 seconds (360 horsepower)
Top speed: 150 miles per hour

$484.20 for the potent 360-horsepower fuel-injected mill.

The '62 model was the best yet, with cleaner lines than before and a reduction of

chrome trim. Under the hood, the Duntov cam installed in the top-shelf fuel-injected engine, which could be revved to an impressive 6,000 rpm, meant that fearsome acceleration was just the flex of an ankle away. Corvettes were filling starting grids on racetracks around the world, garnering positive press, which was used in marketing the car. European sports car makers had to concede that the Corvette was truly world class. And Chevrolet had even better plans on the near horizon. As the Corvette's first generation drew to a close, the 14,531 vehicles sold meant that a second-generation model was inevitable.

Did You Know?

The Sports Car Club of America's A-Production champion in 1962 was dentist Dick Thompson, driving a Corvette. The SCCA's B-Production champ, in a Corvette, was Don Yenko.

Officially, Chevrolet pulled out of racing in 1962, but that didn't mean it didn't go racing. That's what back doors were invented for. Texas Chevrolet dealer/racer Delmo Johnson told Zora Arkus-Duntov that he wanted a real race car. It had to be a winner, and it had to be white. Duntov successfully delivered on both requests.

Equipped with a beefy fuel-injected 327-cubic-inch engine, it was loaded with all the performance options available,

1962 CORVETTE RACE CAR

Price: Unknown (not cheap)

Engine: 360-horsepower, 327-cubic-inch fuel-injected V-8

0–60: 5.0 seconds

Top speed: 165 miles per hour

including 3.36:1 Posi-Traction and RPO 687 heavy-duty suspension and brakes. Then the Corvette was fitted with a full slate of

race components, including a 37.5-gallon fuel tank, headlight covers, a Plexiglas hood deflector, louvers in the hood, and a roll cage, which Chevrolet had packed into a big box and shipped to Texas.

This Corvette competed in scores of races, most significantly finishing third in its A-Production class at the 1962 Sebring 12-hour endurance race. Also in this race car, Johnson and fellow driver David Morgan clinched the SCCA's Southwest Division A-Production championship for 1962. Not bad for a Chevrolet that wasn't supported by the factory. Thank heaven for back doors.

Did You Know?
Rochester Products of Rochester, New York, supplied the Corvette with its mechanical fuel-injection systems from 1957 to 1965.

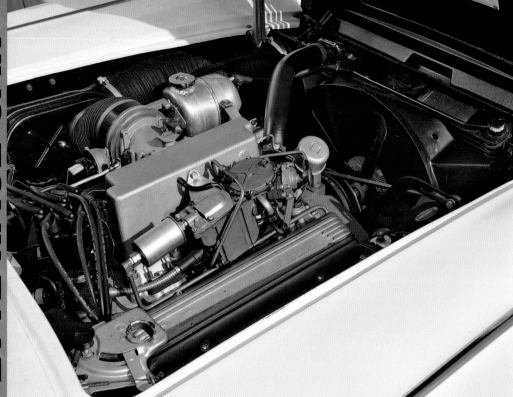

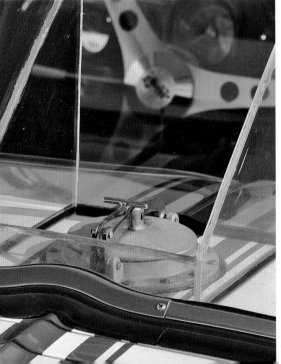

CHAPTER 2
SECOND GENERATION: 1963-1967

Ten years is an eternity in the halls of automobile styling, and the Corvette's first-generation basic design was a decade old by the time its successor hit the showroom. Work on the successor had been underway since 1957, with two internal GM projects—the Q-Corvette and Bill Mitchell's Sting Ray—tapped for inspiration. Elements from both resulted in the XP-720. With a beltline that encircled the car, a long hood, and a tapering, sloping rear, it looked like a drop of water on wheels. The 1959 Sting Ray was a fiberglass-bodied concept car built on the chassis of the 1957 Corvette SS mule—a test bed for engineering and styling ideas, such as inboard brakes, full independent suspension, and fuel injection. Mitchell, who succeeded Harley Earl as the head of GM Design, bought the car from General Motors for $1 and drove it on public roads. The reaction convinced him that the next-generation Corvette would borrow heavily on the Sting Ray's design elements.

When the 1963 Corvette was unveiled, it was a sensation. Jaguar had released the XK-E two years before to wide acclaim, and Chevrolet knew that the second-generation Corvette had to be an over-the-top success. From its electrically actuated hidden headlights to the controversial split rear window, it was an engineering and styling tour de force. The only carryover component from the 1962 Corvette was the 327-cubic-inch V-8 engine. Everything else was new, including the frame, suspension, body, and interior. Even the name was new: Corvette Sting Ray.

Riding on a 98-inch wheelbase, the 1963 Corvette's frame was made of two main longitudinal frame rails connected by crossmembers. While the front suspension was still fully independent, with upper and lower A-arms and coil springs, the rear suspension was all new. It was a clever independent design, with a differential bolted to the frame and with half shafts working with trailing arms and a traverse leaf spring. The suspension was durable and relatively inexpensive. It helped turn the

Corvette into a nimble sports car on the street and the track.

The body design looked like something from a science fiction movie, with dramatic curves, bulges, and vents. Two body styles were offered, a convertible and a stunning coupe, with a center "spine" running the length of the roof, through the rear window, to the graceful tail. Inside the beautiful body was a roomy interior laid out with a full array of gauges and controls. The result was a world-class sports car.

If a flying saucer had landed in Chevrolet showrooms in late 1962, the reaction wouldn't have been far different than the one that greeted the stunning 1963 Corvette Sting Ray Coupe. This was the first coupe in Corvette's history. Designed by the team of Peter Brock, Gene Garfinkle, and Larry Shinoda, under the constant eye of Bill Mitchell, the lines of the Chevy sports car were like nothing else on the road. The dramatic split rear window treatment almost didn't come to fruition, as Mitchell was insistent that the "spine" be left intact, "or else!" The feature lasted one model year.

1963 CORVETTE STING RAY COUPE

Price: $4,682
Engine: 360-horsepower, 327-cubic-inch V-8
0–60: 5.9 seconds
Top speed: 143 miles per hour

As striking as the exterior and interior were, the mechanicals were just as revolutionary, with fully independent suspension, an impressive range of engines, and, for the competitive, the Z06 package. Even the standard Corvette was a taut, well-handling package, able to embarrass European sports cars that cost thousands more. When equipped with the optional fuel-injection system, the Corvette delivered a superb driving experience under all conditions. Customers flocked to Chevrolet showrooms, buying an impressive 21,513 units, almost doubling sales for model year 1963. The car was a masterpiece in 1963 and is still a coveted sports car today.

Did You Know?

One of the rarest options for 1963 was air conditioning. Offered late in the model year, this $421.80 option was installed in just 278 vehicles.

With its roots in the Corvette race cars that preceded it, this Corvette looked as if it were hauling ass when it was sitting still. Under the graceful hood, a wide range of engines could propel the Sting Ray with authority, starting with a 250-horsepower V-8 and topping out with the fire-breathing 360-horse fuel-injected version. The roadster allowed the driver and a passenger to work on their tans when they swung the manual top into the area behind the seats. A fiberglass cover over the folded top maintained the vehicle's sleek lines.

1963 CORVETTE STING RAY ROADSTER

Price: $4,037
Engine (base): 250-horsepower, 327-cubic-inch V-8
0–60: 6.2 seconds
Top speed: 147 miles per hour

A number of styling elements, such as the front fender vents and the grilles atop the hood, were for show only. But these were small matters when the grumble of the powerful engine was floating in the

Corvette's wake. The vast majority (83.5 percent) of Corvettes sold this model year were equipped with a four-speed manual transmission. A long list of options, ranging from "Special Performance Equipment" to backup lights, let buyers create a Sting Ray that reflected their tastes. Chevrolet even offered a removable hardtop, a $236 option that helped turn the Corvette into an (almost) four-season vehicle. The breakdown between the coupe and roadster models was almost 50/50: 10,919 ragtops; 10,594 coupes.

Did You Know?

Early 1963 Corvettes used headlight buckets made of fiberglass, but midway through the model year, they were built out of metal.

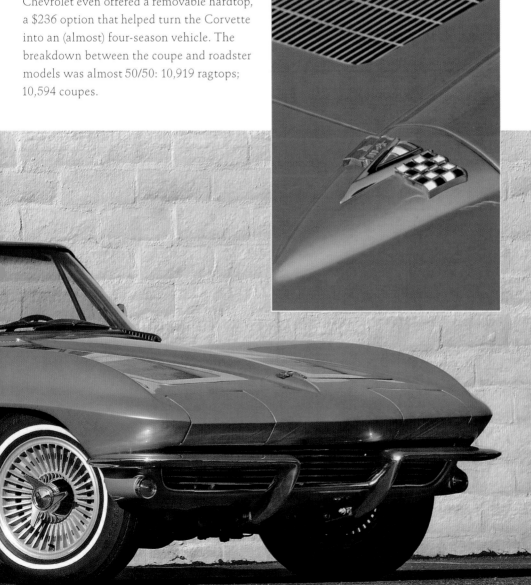

We should all get retirement gifts like this. When Harley J. Earl, the famed General Motors head of styling, stepped away from the reins of power, a grateful Chevrolet built a special Corvette as a way of saying thank you. The special car started life as a red 1963 fuel-injected roadster, but it was shipped to General Motors Design for some nonproduction modifications.

These included special dual dashboard gauge displays, stainless-steel exhaust pipes running from the front fenders into the bespoke side exhaust, interior and exterior trim, and four-wheel disc brakes that were preproduction 1965 components. The exterior was painted Metallic Blue with white trim, while the interior boasted blue leather with

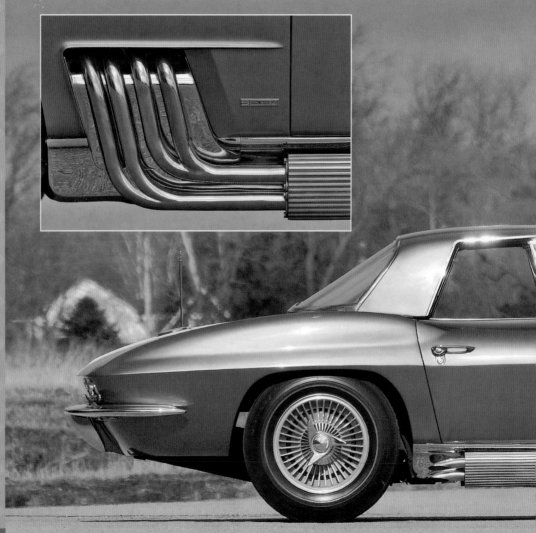

white accents. Today a 300-horsepower, 327-cubic-inch engine is under the hood, as the original engine disappeared.

Two years after he received the car, Earl sold it to a retired U.S. Army veteran. It went through a succession of owners before being sold at the famed Mecum Auction in 2009 for $925,000. Not bad for a free car.

HARLEY EARL'S 1963 CORVETTE ROADSTER

Price (today): $925,000
Engine (current): 300-horsepower, 327-cubic-inch V-8
0–60: 6.0 seconds
Top speed: 130 miles per hour

Did You Know?

Inside a door trim panel was a handwritten number code, "Shop Order 10323," denoting that the car was modified by the craftsmen at General Motors Design.

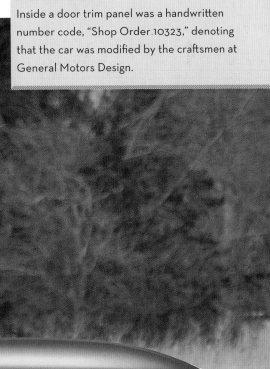

Ever since the mid-1950s, the Corvette had been competing on racetracks around the world, and Chevrolet had been watching and learning. With former racer Zora Arkus-Duntov as the Corvette's chief engineer, the two-seat Chevy had to be able to fight on the track. With the new 1963 version, Duntov and his team put together a turnkey option, RPO Z06 "Special Performance Equipment," targeted at collecting checkered flags. For $1,818.45, a buyer got the performance deal of the decade: special sintered aluminum

1963 CORVETTE STING RAY Z06 COUPE

Price: $6,731
Engine: 360-horsepower, 327-cubic-inch fuel-injected V-8
0–60: 5.0 seconds
Top speed: 160 miles per hour

drum brakes, stiffer front and rear springs, a beefy front anti-sway bar, special shock absorbers, a 36.5-gallon fiberglass fuel tank,

a Kelsey-Hayes dual-circuit master cylinder, and more. It was a flat-out competition package that could be fitted to a street car at the factory. Only 199 of these beasts were built in 1963.

Delmo Johnson was one of the lucky buyers, and he used lessons learned from years of racing to prepare the car for a career of competition. Vents were fitted to the hood. A Plexiglas "fence" installed at the leading edge of the hood generated a low-pressure area above the hood vents to aid in engine cooling. The headlights' electric motors were removed in a bid to reduce weight. These modifications were successful, as the car, with Johnson and David Morgan behind the wheel, placed second in the GTIII class and sixteenth overall at the 1963 Sebring 12-hour endurance race.

Did You Know?
Early aluminum knock-off wheels suffered from a porosity problem. It wasn't until late in the model year that the problem was solved.

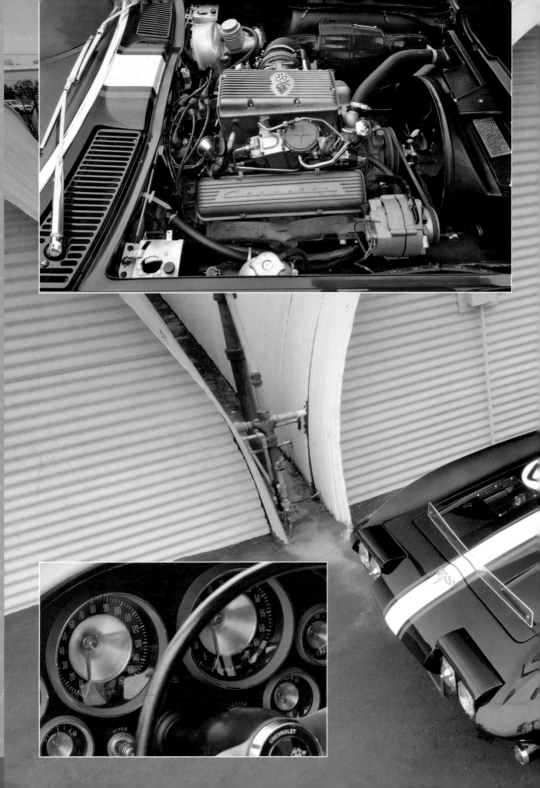

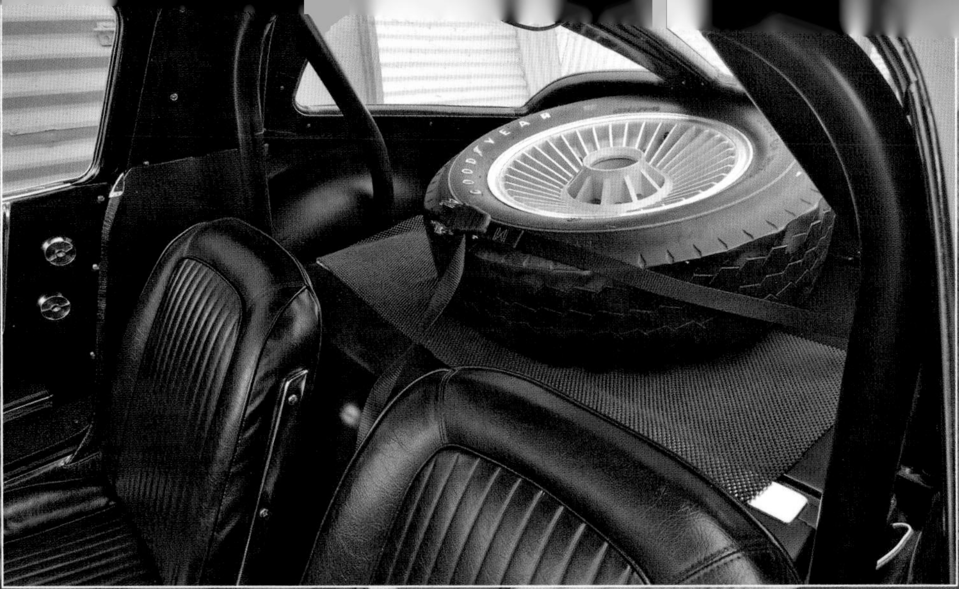
GOODYEAR

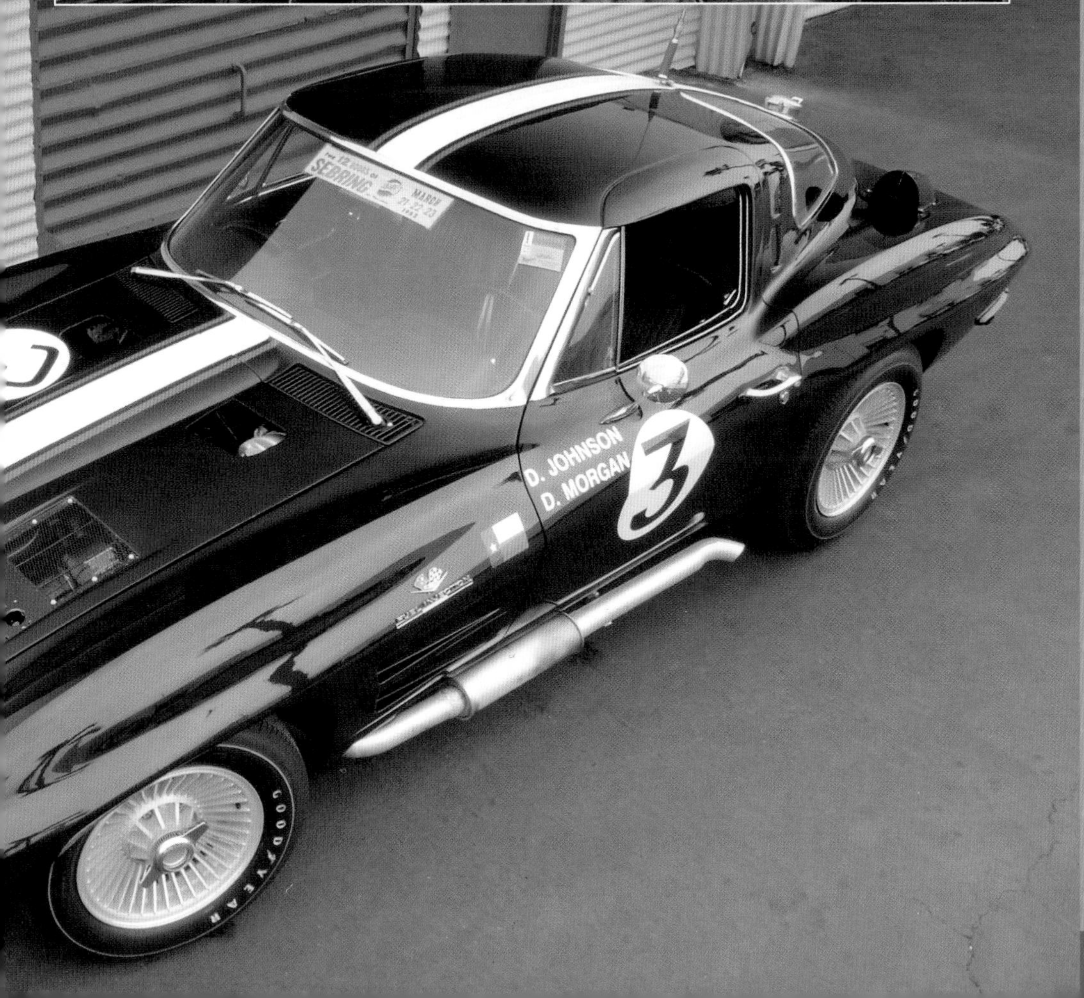
SEBRING
MARCH
D. JOHNSON
D. MORGAN
3
GOODYEAR

This was a transitional year for the midyear Corvettes: it was the first year for four-wheel disc brakes and the last year for a mechanical fuel-injection system. The cost of the fuel-injection option was $538, while the new Mark IV Turbo Jet 396-cubic-inch V-8 cost just $292.70. It was rated at 425 horsepower. For many buyers, the road to tire-melting grunt was easy to see.

Unlike in prior years, the vents behind the front wheels were now functional, allowing hot engine compartment air to exit. The hood no longer had depressions on it:

small-block-equipped Corvettes had smooth hoods. But fuel-injection-equipped cars such as this still wore an identification badge above the side vents. With the lightweight

1965 CORVETTE STING RAY ROADSTER, FUEL INJECTED

Price: $4,644
Engine: 375-horsepower, 327-cubic-inch fuel-injected V-8
0–60: 6.2 seconds
Top speed: 148 miles per hour

small-block engine cranking out 375 horsepower and with disc brakes on every corner, the 1965 Corvette was a capable canyon carver, as well as a superb long-distance tourer. Sales were good, and 15,378 of the 23,564 Corvettes built in model year 1965 were convertibles.

Though four-wheel disc brakes were standard, buyers who wanted drum brakes on their 1965 Corvettes (while supplies lasted) received a credit of $64.50. A total of 316 Corvettes were fitted with the remaining brake components.

Did You Know?

Chevrolet projected that the front brake pads in the new disc brake system would last 57,000 miles.

Chevrolet kept changes to the Corvette to a minimum for 1966, at least externally. A different grille pattern was evident, as was a changed, more upright script on the Corvette badging. The backup lights were now standard. But this was a Corvette in the 1960s, and buyers were more interested in pushing the front of the sports car through the air than seeing behind them. For 1966, the Mark IV V-8 engine,

displacing 396 inches in 1965, enjoyed an increase in displacement to 427. Zora Arkus-Duntov sold the idea of enlarging the engine to the brass at Chevrolet by telling them that the increase in bore resulted in a lighter engine, thus improving fuel economy. And they bought it!

Actually, quite a few customers bought the big-block engine in 1966: 10,375. Of that sum, 5,258 sprang the $312.85 for

RPO L72, putting 425 healthy ponies in front of the firewall. This reciprocating grenade could hurl the Corvette down the length of a drag strip in the 11-second range, depending on the rear axle ratio. With a vehicle weight of only 3,140 pounds and with the massive power of Chevrolet's "Rat" engine, under heavy throttle, the driver's attention was firmly focused on the view through the windshield.

1966 CORVETTE STING RAY ROADSTER

Price: $4,684
Engine: 425-horsepower, 427-cubic-inch V-8
0–60: 4.8 seconds
Top speed: 140 miles per hour

Did You Know?

If you wanted a big-block under the hood, you had to have a few mandatory options: Posi-Traction and a close-ratio Muncie four-speed manual transmission.

It's good to be the boss—or the boss's spouse. When you are the head of General Motors Design, it's possible to have something special created for your wife. This is exactly what Bill Mitchell did for his bride, Marian. By using a Central Office Production Order (COPO), it was possible to build special vehicles not normally seen in showrooms. Marian wanted a convertible equipped with an automatic transmission, but being the wife of Bill Mitchell, she got a whole lot more. Zora Arkus-Duntov filled

MRS. WILLIAM MITCHELL'S 1967 CORVETTE STING RAY ROADSTER

Price: N/A
Engine: 390-horsepower, 427-cubic-inch V-8
0–60: 6.1 seconds
Top speed: 146 miles per hour

a memo book with instructions for the assembly line regarding the car's build. Bill walked the vehicle down the assembly line himself, ensuring that the big-block engine,

as well as virtually every option available, was installed properly. Then the car was taken to the General Motors Technical Center, where more custom touches were fitted. These included red accents applied to sill panels, front and rear wheelwells, rear interior trim panels, and suspension components. Then a full-length red stripe was painted onto the Ermine White finish.

Marian Mitchell drove the car for two years, quite a long time for a household that saw a never-ending stream of interesting vehicles. It has since gone through a succession of owners who have respected its history. In 2001, it was the first Corvette to be given the prestigious Bloomington Gold Historic Award.

Did You Know?

In 1967, Corvettes equipped with the 427/390 engine, an automatic transmission, and air conditioning had their front license plates fitted beneath the driver side bumper to allow more cooling air to hit the radiator.

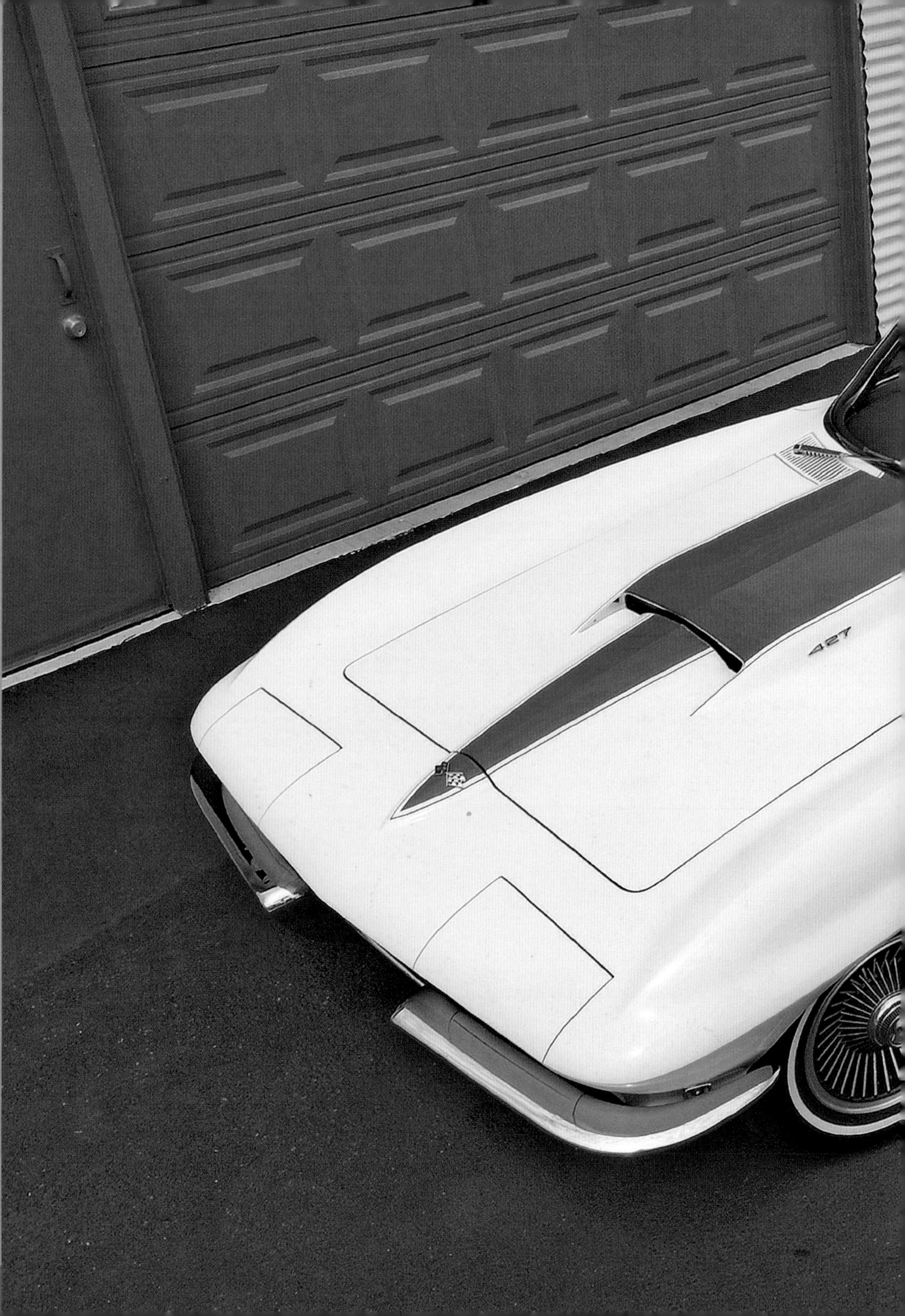
427

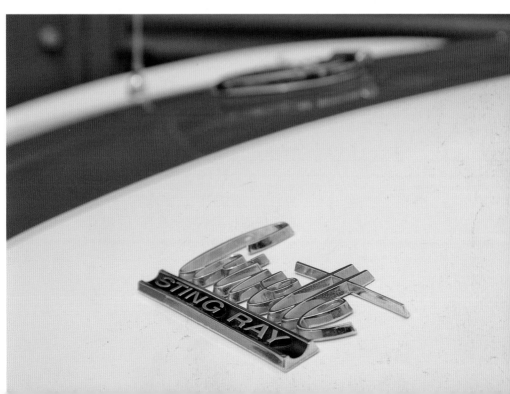

When the second-generation Corvette debuted, its huge wraparound rear window was a two-piece affair. A center "spine" ran the length of the vehicle. But over Bill Mitchell's protests, the rear window became one piece in 1964. By the last year of the generation, everyone had embraced the sleek lines of the large piece of glass.

They also embraced the potent engines that could be fitted beneath the hood, especially the big-block variants. While

1967 CORVETTE STING RAY COUPE

Price: $4,588
Engine: 390-horsepower, 427-cubic-inch V-8
0–60: 5.9 seconds
Top speed: 143 miles per hour

the 435-horse version got all the press, for day-in, day-out trouble-free driving, it was hard to beat the 390-horsepower

offering. With hydraulic lifters, it was low maintenance and was a bit quieter than the higher-powered mills. Air conditioning was available with the entry-level big-block, and an automatic transmission was a viable way to shift gears.

But make no mistake, it could still run with the big dogs. With 460 lb-ft of torque on tap, there wasn't a street tire on the market that was safe from being transformed into a cloud of smoke with a simple push of the accelerator. And RPO L36 cost only $200.15. I don't see a downside at all.

Did You Know?
A dual system brake master cylinder debuted on the 1967 Corvette, giving the sports car an added level of safety.

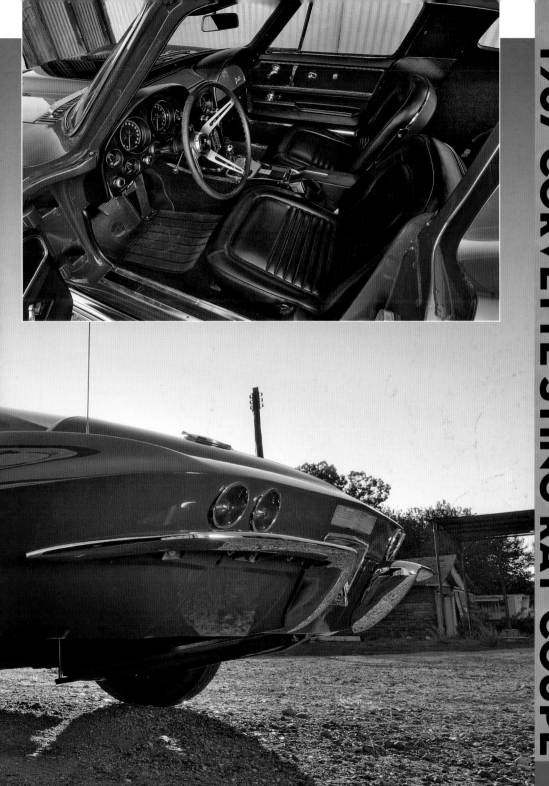

What we have here are bookends, two cars that show the wide range of options available to Corvette buyers at the time. The blue ragtop was equipped with a base 327-cubic-inch engine and a moderate number of options, while the silver car packed an L89 big-block beneath the hood.

The blue roadster was equipped with a 300-horsepower engine and a normal load of options, such as an AM/FM radio, power steering, a telescopic wheel, and tinted windows. A buyer could enjoy the Corvette lifestyle without breaking the bank buying the car or insuring it.

For drivers who had velocity on their minds, a big-block engine under the hood gave the pilot instant street cred. With 427 cubic inches and RPO L89 aluminum heads, the silver car demanded respect at all times. The alloy heads were an

attempt to bring the weight down on the front wheels, making the car more competitive. The option was priced at $368.65, and only 16 Corvettes were thus equipped. The aggressive-looking (and -sounding) factory side exhaust set a buyer back $131.65, but the snarl from those long pipes made them worth every penny. As evidenced here, there was a Corvette for every purse and purpose.

1967 CORVETTE STING RAY ROADSTERS

Price: $5,028 (327); $5,780 (427)
Engine: 300-horsepower, 327-cubic-inch V-8; 435-horsepower, 427-cubic-inch V-8
0–60: 7.8 seconds (327); 5.5 seconds (427)
Top speed: 131 miles per hour (327); 143 miles per hour (427)

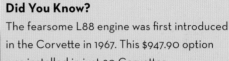

Did You Know?
The fearsome L88 engine was first introduced in the Corvette in 1967. This $947.90 option was installed in just 20 Corvettes.

CHAPTER 3
THIRD GENERATION, 1968-1982

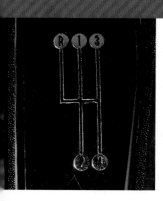

After five years in showrooms, the Corvette Sting Ray was replaced by an even swoopier design, as if that were possible. Design chief Bill Mitchell was at the height of his power, and with his firm hand and superb sense of style, the Corvette blossomed into a vehicle that influenced designers around the world. The visual echoes of this stunning design are even visible in contemporary Corvettes. The styling was that strong.

Before the revolutionary 1963 Corvette Sting Ray had started production, Mitchell called his designers together and told them to start work on the next model Corvette. He intended the Sting Ray to be built for three years—four years, tops. A worthy successor had to be ready to pick up the baton.

Mitchell had a lot of Corvette concept cars built over the years, and unlike most show cars, his were actual streetable vehicles. One of his favorites was the 1965 Mako Shark II, a low-slung missile built on a C2 chassis but with exaggerated fenders, a chiseled nose, and dramatic sloping rear pillars. Designed by Larry Shinoda, two were built, and they would show what the future of the Corvette looked like. With a tapered midsection nicknamed a "Coke bottle" and a far more aerodynamic front end than the midyear models, the car looked fast just sitting still.

Chevrolet's production studio, headed by Hank Haga, was tasked with turning a wild concept car into a street-legal, and livable, automobile. Using the chassis under the midyear models, the studio was able to (slightly) tame the over-the-top contours into a Corvette that would pass all requirements. As with its generational predecessor, the headlights were hidden, but now they were raised and lowered via a vacuum system. The windshield wipers lived under a small vacuum-operated door, giving the third-generation Corvette, or C3, a cleaner look.

One problem with the C2 models was their tendency to lift off the road at high speed. Zora Arkus-Duntov described the C2's aerodynamics as being "like a really bad wing." When you're rocketing along at triple digits, the last thing you want is the front end to lift. To combat this tendency, the new C3 Corvette's sloping nose was designed to keep the front tires in contact with the road at high speeds. Unfortunately, a small ducktail spoiler at the rear was very effective, pushing the back of the car down at speed, thus lifting the front. Duntov put a small chin spoiler beneath the grille, and this cured the problem to some extent.

With the new C3 Corvette built on the carryover C2 chassis, the powertrains were pretty much carried over as well. Both small- and big-block V-8s were slipped between the graceful front fenders, and the large engines lived under a bulging hood. Very dramatic.

Duntov was heavily into racing, and the C3 was a great platform for assaulting racetracks around the world. In 1969, buyers could even get a factory-built Corvette with the fearsome ZL1 all-aluminum 427-cubic-inch engine, delivering more than 550 horsepower. With the reduction in weight over the front end, the car handled better. And with the race-bred powerplant, it was ready for very high-speed endurance racing. Two examples were built, and both survive to this day.

But the vast majority of Corvette customers took home a wickedly beautiful automobile that they could live with every day. Former General Motors design head Harley Earl would tell his designers, "If you go by a schoolyard, and kids don't whistle, back to the drawing board." The third-generation Corvette collected whistles.

THIRD GENERATION, 1968-1982

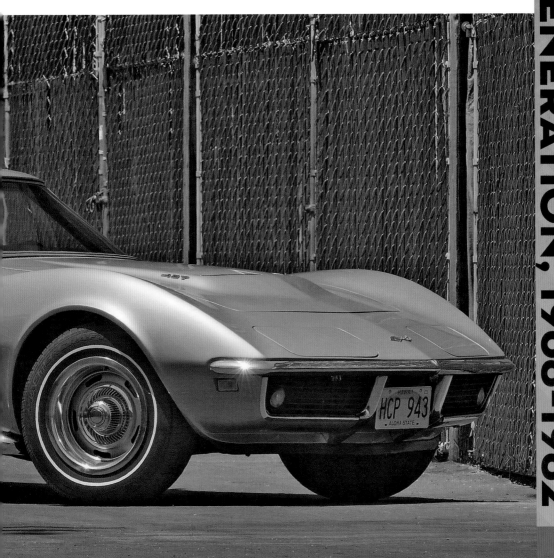

For buyers in 1968 who just had to have the strongest Corvette on the road, there was only one choice: RPO L88. This big-block-engine option required a slew of mandatory options to accompany it, including the F41 suspension, J56 heavy-duty brakes, and a Posi-Traction rear end. The engine used 103-octane fuel, aluminum heads, and a 12.5:1 compression to generate a staggering amount of power. Officially, this powerplant was rated at 430 horsepower for insurance

1968 CORVETTE L88 CONVERTIBLE

Price: $6,800
Engine: 430-horsepower, 427-cubic-inch V-8
0–60: 5.9 seconds
Top speed: 170 miles per hour

purposes. Sure, it made 435 ponies—on its way to 560 horses. The L88 was a race engine in a street car, pure and simple.

Such performance didn't come cheap. RPO L88 cost $947.90, and that was just for the engine. Add up the required options, and the cost climbed as fast as the car under heavy throttle. This kept the L88 a rare beast, as only 80 were built in 1968, and 20 of those were convertibles. Because it was a (very) thinly disguised race car, the L88 lacked a number of features missing that were standard on "normal" Corvettes: there was no radio offered, and there was no shield around the engine fan. Shielding helped direct cooling air through the radiator at low speeds. The L88 was built for continuous high speeds—as found on a racetrack.

Did You Know?

The air filter for the L88 was actually mounted on the underside of the hood, not attached to the top of the engine.

29

When the sophomore C3s hit the streets, customers found a Corvette that enjoyed a slew of improvements. It's often said that the little things can make or break a car, and Chevrolet took pains to correct the little things—such as new interior door panels that gave occupants an additional 1/2 inch of shoulder room on each side, a steering wheel that was 1 inch smaller in diameter, and an ignition switch moved from the dashboard to the steering wheel. The push-button exterior door handles were replaced with push-down flaps, and the name Stingray returned to the Corvette, though now it was one word.

Under the hood, the small-block engine grew in displacement to 350 cubic inches, helping power levels remain constant under the growing mechanical demands of

emissions control equipment. The big-blocks were unchanged, meaning that it was child's play to scare oneself witless in the blink of an eye. One head-turning option that debuted in 1969 was a new side exhaust system. With its deep-throated grumble and race-ready looks, it gave the Corvette an air of menace. For Corvette buyers, this was not a bad thing.

1969 CORVETTE STINGRAY COUPE

Price: $5,470
Engine: 435-horsepower, 427-cubic-inch V-8
0–60: 6.5 seconds
Top speed: 142 miles per hour

Did You Know?

Manual transmissions were a lot more popular in 1969: 78.4 percent of Corvettes that year were so equipped.

It was the dogs. Motion Performance founder Joel Rosen liked to travel with his dogs. So when he was designing the wild Motion GT Corvette, he made sure that the area under the sloping rear window was big enough for his pets.

Being a Motion Performance product, though, it sure didn't run like a dog. With a blueprinted Phase III 454 under the hood, this engine was rated at 535 horsepower. Behind the potent big-block was a modified Turbo HydraMatic 400 automatic

1970 MOTION GT 454 CORVETTE

Price: $13,000

Engine: 535-horsepower, 454-cubic-inch V-8

0–60: 4.4 seconds

Top speed: More than 150 miles per hour

transmission, with a Hone overdrive unit downstream. This transformed the 4.88:1 rear axle ratio, ideal for sprinting off the line, into a more highway-cruising-friendly

3.42:1 gear ratio. So the Motion GT Corvette could launch as though it were coming off an aircraft carrier's catapult, then cruise like a Boeing 747.

The outrageous bodywork was designed by Rosen to make a statement. The huge headers feeding a side exhaust system big enough to hide small pets weren't there just for show; when a 454 engine is in full song, it needs to breathe. While Motion Performance sold only a handful of GT Corvettes, it sold *a lot* of body kits, giving customers the opportunity to transform their Corvettes into lookalikes. But the real Motion GT 454s could run with the biggest dogs. Just bring money.

Did You Know?
Motion Performance engineered the Motion GT 454 to have an effective air conditioning system, despite the car having well over 500 horsepower.

By 1974, brute performance was on its way out, thanks to federal emissions regulations and rising insurance premiums. These forces had combined to seal the fate of huge-displacement engines cranking out obscene levels of power. The emphasis was now on delivering a high-quality motoring experience. The Corvette, always a good-handling sports car, raised the level of cornering prowess. Noise, vibration, and harshness (NVH) were tackled in an effort

1974 CORVETTE STINGRAY ROADSTER

Price: $6,064
Engine: 250-horsepower, 350-cubic-inch V-8
0–60: 7.5 seconds
Top speed: 124 miles per hour

to reduce long-distance discomfort, with considerable success, but the situation in the engine room was radically different from a couple of years prior.

Two engines were still available, the 350- and 454-cubic-inch units, but they were a shadow of years past. The top-rated small-block cranked out just 250 horses, while the big-block served up only 270 ponies. This would be the last year for the 454, as ever-more-stringent emissions regs would doom the powerplant.

Externally, the Corvette changed, particularly the rear end. Federal impact regulations now required new vehicles to be equipped at each end with bumpers that could withstand 5-mile-per-hour impacts. The crew at Corvette created a smooth, tasteful solution. Of course, when you're in a Corvette convertible, wind in the hair and sun on the face, all is well.

Did You Know?

This was the last year for the Corvette to use leaded fuel. Catalytic converters were fitted for 1975, necessitating the use of unleaded gasoline.

End of an era. This was the last Baldwin-Motion car ever built. Equipped with a mighty L88 427-cubic-inch engine, long after Chevrolet was putting these monsters into street cars, Motion Performance had to admit that terrifyingly fast sports cars were no longer in demand. It didn't help that even a small manufacturer like Motion couldn't skirt federal regulations. The company was finding more of a demand for its Chevrolet Vegas, stuffed with a massaged 454.

1974 BALDWIN-MOTION L88 PHASE III CORVETTE COUPE

Price: $8,600
Engine: 600-horsepower, 427-cubic-inch V-8
0–60: 4.9 seconds
Top speed: 144 miles per hour

This beast was originally ordered by a dealer of exotic cars in New England. Equipped with the huge powerplant, its

power was fed through a manual four-speed transmission using a Hurst shifter. Being part of a Motion Performance vehicle, the L88 engine couldn't be left alone. Heavily modified, it generated staggering amount of power. Chromed tubular headers dumped the exhaust fumes into a pair of side-mounted pipes. The resulting audio carnage set off car alarms at 30 paces.

The problem driving this automobile is twofold: keeping one's foot off the accelerator and hoping the rear tires hook up when you do succumb to temptation. The last Baldwin-Motion vehicle went out on a high note.

Did You Know?
Baldwin Chevrolet was located down the street from Motion Performance. Customers would buy cars at Baldwin and take them to Motion for modifications.

For Corvette, 1975 was not a year of radical change. Rather it was a year of a refinement. Externally, the most visible indication of change was the rear bumper cover being a one-piece molding, unlike the two-piece affair of 1974. Both front and rear bumpers had vertical pads molded in, an attempt to minimize the scuffing of light contact.

Under the fiberglass skin lay bigger changes. The big-block engine was no longer offered. In fact, only one optional engine was available, RPO L82. Rated at

1975 CORVETTE STINGRAY COUPE

Price: $7,540
Engine: 205-horsepower, 350-cubic-inch V-8
0–60: 7.7 seconds
Top speed: 129 miles per hour

205 horsepower, it, like the base 165-horse engine, breathed through a catalytic converter. Exhaust gases were directed to a single converter. Then a pair of pipes led to

the dual exhaust tips. High-energy ignition (HEI) appeared in the Corvette for the first time in 1975, but it was the last year for "Astro Ventilation." It had not worked as well as engineers had hoped, so it was pulled. This year was the last one that saw a production Corvette convertible offered. The ragtop wouldn't return to the scene until 1988. Despite the reduction in power, the Corvette was popular: 38,465 were sold in model year 1975—an increase over the preceding year.

Did You Know?
This was the first year since 1964 that the Corvette had only a single engine displacement.

In the mid-1970s, one of the top race series in the United States was run by the International Motor Sports Association (IMSA). At the time, one of the most competitive classes in IMSA was filled with race cars wearing wild bodywork and packing huge engines. Motion Performance was never known to let a trend pass by untouched. To respond to the call for IMSA-like vehicles, it built the Motion Spyder Coupe.

This example is the prototype. It is fitted with huge fender extensions typical of IMSA race cars, and both front and rear bumper caps have been heavily modified. The headlights are housed in fixed, recessed cavities. Under the hood, a huge 466-cubic-inch engine gave the Corvette race car–like punch. The installation of a hone overdrive unit, its control lever mounted on the right side of the center tunnel next to a passenger's knee, allowed the Motion Spyder to eat

long-distance miles without the engine turning over at a frightful rpm.

A tuck-and-roll upholstery treatment gave the interior a custom touch. With the outrageous paint scheme, burly exhaust note, and take-no-prisoners looks, the Spyder was never mistaken for anything but a race car for the street. Unfortunately, with the gas crisis of the 1970s, demand kept production to just four cars.

1976 MOTION CAN-AM SPYDER PROTOTYPE COUPE

Price: $12,500
Engine: 610-horsepower, 466-cubic-inch V-8
0–60: 3.8 seconds
Top speed: 156 miles per hour

Did You Know?
Motion Performance's founder, Joel Rosen, raced straight-axle Corvettes in hillclimbs and road races early in his career.

Chevrolet has always enjoyed birthdays, and to celebrate the Corvette's 25th, the car was given a significant makeover and tapped to pace the annual Indianapolis 500. This was the first time a Corvette would pace the historic race, and Chevrolet gave the sports car its biggest freshening since 1968. A large rear window was installed, greatly increasing cargo-carrying ability, and the entire interior enjoyed a reworking. Power was increased from prior years, giving the entire Corvette range better acceleration

1978 CORVETTE PACE CAR REPLICA

Price: $13,653
Engine: 220-horsepower, 350-cubic-inch V-8
0–60: 6.6 seconds
Top speed: 127 miles per hour

while maintaining fuel economy. The optional P255/60R15 tires were so wide that assembly line workers in St. Louis, Missouri, had to hand-trim the wheel openings to provide sufficient clearance.

Chevrolet planned to build 300 replicas of the actual pace car, with its dramatic black over silver paint, but demand for the model forced Chevy to build one for every dealer, as well as a few hundred spares. Final production of the Pace Car Replica was 6,502 units.

The two-tone paint was so popular that Chevrolet reversed it, with silver on top and gray below the beltline, calling it the Silver Anniversary Edition. Available on all 1978 Corvettes were new options, including an AM/FM radio with a CB. The citizens band radio craze was sweeping the nation, and now Corvette drivers could bellow out a big "10-4, Good Buddy!"

Did You Know?

Jim Rathmann, the 1960 Indy 500 winner, drove the actual pace car during the 1978 race.

OFFICIAL PACE CAR

62nd ANNUAL INDIANAPOLIS 500 MILE RACE

MAY 28, 1978

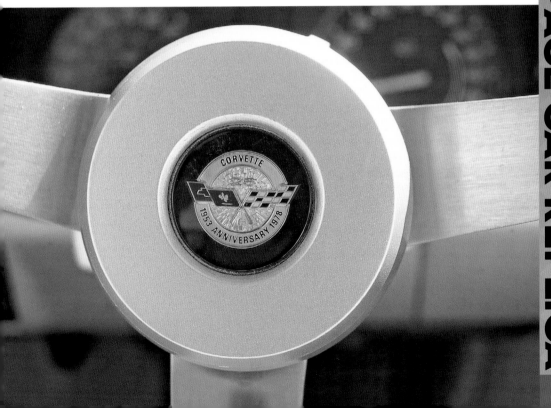

What Chevrolet giveth, Chevrolet taketh away. For the final year of the C3, the Corvette was given a new type of induction system, called Cross Fire Fuel Injection. It improved overall drivability, improved mileage, and added 10 horsepower. Yet all that good news was tempered by the fact that no manual transmission was offered. One engine, one gearbox, period.

Under the curvaceous body was a new fiberglass leaf spring in the rear suspension, replacing the heavy multileaf steel spring

1982 CORVETTE COUPE

Price: $18,290
Engine: 200-horsepower, 350-cubic-inch V-8
0–60: 7.9 seconds
Top speed: 123 miles per hour

in use since 1963. The sole transmission was a four-speed automatic, with a torque converter clutch in the top four gears. This was used to improve fuel mileage and to reduce interior noise at highway speeds.

Chevrolet used the C3's last year to release the Collector Edition. With a special paint-and-graphics package, it introduced a lifting rear window to the Corvette world. This feature would be standard on most future Corvettes, and the ease of access to the storage area was an instant hit. The Collector Edition was the first Corvette to break the $20,000 mark; it took $22,537.59 to put one in the garage. Only 6,759 were built, with total Corvette sales at 25,407 that year. This was the first full year of production at the all-new Corvette assembly plant in Bowling Green, Kentucky.

Did You Know?

Nine new 1982 Corvettes were sold to customers in Japan, while sales to Canada were 459 units.

CHAPTER 4
FOURTH GENERATION, 1984-1996

The Corvette faithful had been pining for an all-new Corvette for many years. Rumors of a mid-engined 'Vette had been swirling around in magazines, and Chevrolet did little to dispel the whispers. But the truth was that the Corvette in the early 1980s was showing its age. Beneath the svelte contours lay the same frame design found under Corvettes in 1963. The underpinnings had enjoyed continuous technological improvements, especially in the area of tires. But a simple ladder frame can be improved only so far, and Corvette engineers had big plans for the future. These plans required a fresh approach, from frame to fenders.

Older Corvettes had a disconcerting tendency to lift the nose at high speed. With the advent of fuel injection, the Corvette's engine could propel the sports car deep into triple-digit territory. An increased awareness of the importance of aerodynamic styling now flowed through Chevrolet design, and the 1984 Corvette enjoyed the fruits of these labors. With its chiseled nose, steeply raked windshield, restrained lines, and abrupt tail, the Corvette could now break 150 miles per hour without breaking a sweat. While some traditional Corvette styling cues, such as hidden headlights, broad front fenders, and circular tail lamps, were retained, most of the design was fresh.

The interior of the 1984 Corvette broke with tradition as much as the exterior did. No longer did long needles swing across the face of a speedometer and a tachometer; liquid crystal technology had now come to the instrument panel. Colorful bar graphics showed the driver engine revs, while a digital readout displayed how much the speed limit was being abused. Nicknamed "Tokyo at night," the display was configurable to the driver's wishes.

But the most revolutionary aspect of the newest Corvette, the fourth generation, or C4, wasn't visible unless you were beneath the car. The suspension was all new, built of aluminum, and attached to a partial unit body. Both front and rear suspensions utilized transverse fiberglass leaf springs, helping the C4 attain a lateral g of 0.95, a record for a street car.

Another record was the angle on the windshield, a very steep 64 degrees. Stylist John Cafaro penned the overall design, including the huge clamshell hood, which opened to expose the entire engine and front suspension. Considerable effort was taken to integrate all the mechanical bits under the hood, giving the production car a race car–like appearance in the engine compartment.

With the stress on aerodynamics, the C4 Corvette was destined for high speeds. But a sports car is only as good as its tires. Chevrolet

worked closely with Goodyear to create rolling stock that could withstand very high speeds in all weather conditions while delivering a (relatively) quiet and smooth ride. The Goodyear Gatorbacks set a new level of streetable performance. It was like having your cake and eating it too.

The press loved the car, calling it the world's finest sports car. The public felt the same way, signing sales contracts in record numbers. While many within General Motors had expressed reservations about the need for a new Corvette, the hard-core within the company knew it was time. They pressed ahead on it, and the result was world class.

It didn't take another 25 years for the Corvette to be found at the head of the grid at the Indianapolis 500. With the release of the C4, Chevrolet provided a new Corvette, to be driven by fighter ace and test pilot legend Chuck Yeager. Unlike the previous Corvette pace car, this year's version was a convertible. The ragtop returned, having been off the menu since 1976. For only the second time in the history of the Indy 500, a street-legal vehicle was the pace car, needing

1986 CORVETTE PACE CAR REPLICA CONVERTIBLE

Price: $32,032
Engine: 230-horsepower, 5.7-liter V-8
0–60: 5.7 seconds
Top speed: 150 miles per hour

no modifications to carry out its pacing duties. The only other automobile that had required zero changes to fulfill its pace car job was the 1978 Corvette.

Federal requirements said that starting in 1986, all automobiles sold in the United States had to be equipped with a center, high-mounted stop light (CHMSL). The Corvette convertible mounted its CHMSL in the rear bumper cap. Another first for the Corvette in 1986 was the adoption of standard anti-lock brakes (ABS). Under the hood now lived true tuned port fuel injection, introduced in 1985. Performance enthusiasts loved it.

Did You Know?
For a sports car as technically advanced as the 1986 Corvette, 166 were built with the radio deleted from the factory.

INDIANAPOLIS 500 — 70th — MAY 25, 1986

TUNED PORT INJECTION

It didn't take Chevrolet long to realize that with the continued production of the Corvette now spanning multiple decades, the anniversaries were coming fast and furious. The car's 35th birthday was celebrated with a coupe-only package, RPO Z01, the 35th Anniversary Special Edition. Costing $4,795, the option resulted in a Corvette that looked as if it had been dipped in a vat of white paint. From the white wheels to the white steering wheel, it was an auto detailer's nightmare. Special 35th anniversary logos were found on the front fenders, the headrests, and a numbered badge on the center console.

With such a lofty price, the option was limited to buyers with deep pockets. Production of the RPO was 2,050 units. Part of the package was a revised exhaust system with reduced-restriction mufflers,

giving the car a more aggressive growl, as well as kicking the power up by five ponies. Every 35th Anniversary Edition Corvette packed a 3.07:1 gear set in the differential. The removable roof panel was held on by bolts that could be tightened and loosened with a special wrench that came with the car. Bolting the roof panel onto the vehicle structure improved the structural rigidity of the Corvette, giving it superior handling.

1988 CORVETTE 35TH ANNIVERSARY EDITION

Price: $34,284
Engine: 245-horsepower, 5.7-liter V-8
0-60: 5.4 seconds
Top speed: 154 miles per hour

Did You Know?

Total Corvette production for 1988 was 22,789—15,382 coupes and 7,407 convertibles.

All it took was checking a box on the order form: "Regular Production Option B2K." Oh, and writing a sizable check. But what you got was nothing short of stunning. It was the only time that Chevrolet gave an outsider an RPO. But then, this was no ordinary Corvette.

Reeves Callaway had a history of extracting maximum reliable horsepower from an engine, often by using forced induction, such as turbocharging. This is

1990 CALLAWAY TWIN TURBO CORVETTE

Price: $58,874
Engine: 390-horsepower, 5.7-liter V-8
0–60: 5.1 seconds
Top speed: 191 miles per hour

the approach he took to create an uber-performing Corvette. Two turbos, breathing through a pair of intercoolers, transformed the sporty Corvette into a street-legal

monster. But a civilized monster. Customers ordered the car from select dealers. Then a Corvette would be sent down the Bowling Green assembly line. After that, it would be drop-shipped to Callaway's facility in Old Lyme, Connecticut, where the go-fast bits would be installed. This road rocket sold in sufficient numbers (58 in 1990) to keep the doors open at Callaway. Buyers wanting to go shiftless could order an automatic for an additional $6,500. This slush box was a massaged truck Turbo HydraMatic 400, tough enough to handle the 562 lb-ft of torque. Regardless of what transmission was used, the result was the same: mind-bending performance.

Did You Know?
The Callaway Twin Turbo enjoyed a full factory warranty, except for the powertrain, which Callaway covered for 12,000 miles or 12 months, whichever came first.

It had been promised to arrive in 1989, but it didn't come onto the scene until 1990. It was debuted to the world's press at the 1989 Geneva Auto Show, and the question on everyone's mind was, worth the wait? Boy howdy! This was a Corvette that could go head to head with the world's best sports cars and kick most of them into the weeds. The Lotus-designed four-cam, all-aluminum V-8 displaced 5.7 liters and was a veritable fire-breather built by Mercury Marine in Stillwater, Oklahoma. Designated the LT5, the hand-built powerplant used 32 valves to breathe.

A number of subtle body modifications visually set the 1990 ZR-1 apart from plain-Jane Corvettes. These included a convex rear bumper cap, rear quarter panel flares, and very

discreet badging. Built from 1990 through 1995, the ZR-1 was dubbed King of the Hill, and its ability to rocket down a drag strip in 13.1 seconds at 110 miles per hour showed that the moniker was justified. Any transmission was available for use with the ZR-1, as long as it was the Borg-Warner six-speed manual. The RPO for the ZR-1 was $27,016. That's just the cost of the option alone!

1990 CORVETTE ZR-1

Price: $58,995
Engine: 375-horsepower, 5.7-liter V-8
0–60: 4.7 seconds
Top speed: 180 miles per hour

Did You Know?

Despite its hefty price, 3,049 ZR-1s were built for model year 1990. In its six-year production run, 6,939 ZR-1s were constructed.

One dozen. That's all that were built. Granted, they weren't inexpensive. But the lucky buyers got one hell of a lot of technology. The L98 5.7-liter engine was treated to a pair of Garrett Rotomaster T04 turbochargers, feeding high test into the cylinders via multipoint fuel injection. Bolted to the back of the engine was a ZF six-speed manual transmission. All of these bits worked together to hurl the Speedster down a drag strip in just 12.7 seconds.

1991 CALLAWAY SPEEDSTER

Price: $150,000
Engine: 450-horsepower, 5.7-liter V-8
0-60: 4.2 seconds
Top speed: 190 miles per hour

But this vehicle's forte was road work. Reeves Callaway was a successful race car driver, and he demanded that any car wearing his name was a capable canyon

carver as well as a straight-line missile. With its huge four-wheel Brembo disc brakes and leech-like 18-inch Bridgestone Potenza tires, the Speedster responded like a slot car. With the interior redesign that the entire Corvette line enjoyed in 1990, the Callaway's occupants enjoyed surroundings as upscale as the rest of the car. Designer Paul Deutschman and Callaway created a lowered windshield, intending that the Speedster be enjoyed on sunny days. That's why the vehicle debuted at the Los Angeles Auto Show. It was an appropriate setting for such a spectacular vehicle.

Did You Know?
Prior to being installed in the Speedster, the engines were blueprinted and fitted with Cosworth pistons and forged crankshafts.

When you spend your youth racing cars, you don't settle for a "conventional" vehicle to put your name on. Dick Guldstrand started racing when straight-axle Corvettes were new, and as the car evolved, Guldstrand moved up the ranks, piloting Grand Sports into history. In the 1980s, Dick released a Corvette-based car called the GS80, which ran like a street-legal race car but looked nearly stock. When the ZR-1 debuted in

1994 GULDSTRAND GS90

Price: $206,208
Engine: 475-horsepower, 5.7-liter V-8
0–60: 3.9 seconds
Top speed: 182 miles per hour

1990, Guldstrand decided to build another car with his name on it, but it wouldn't look like a stock Corvette. A Corvette suspension

guru, Dick had assisted Chevrolet in developing the C4's underpinnings. He took all his experience and created the GS90.

With slippery bodywork, a massaged ZR-1 engine, and a Guldstrand-tweaked suspension, it looked like a street-legal race car and moved as though it were track ready. While the body was based on a C4 Corvette, the only stock bits from the Corvette were the windshield and side glass.

Only six GS90s were built; Chevrolet didn't take kindly to Guldstrand stepping on the ZR-1's toes and soon pulled the plug on the program. (I suspect that the price of the car might have had something to do with its short production run as well.)

Did You Know?

The Nassau Blue paint scheme with the broad white stripe paid homage to the original Corvette Grand Sports, which Guldstrand had spent time racing.

1994 GULDSTRAND GS90

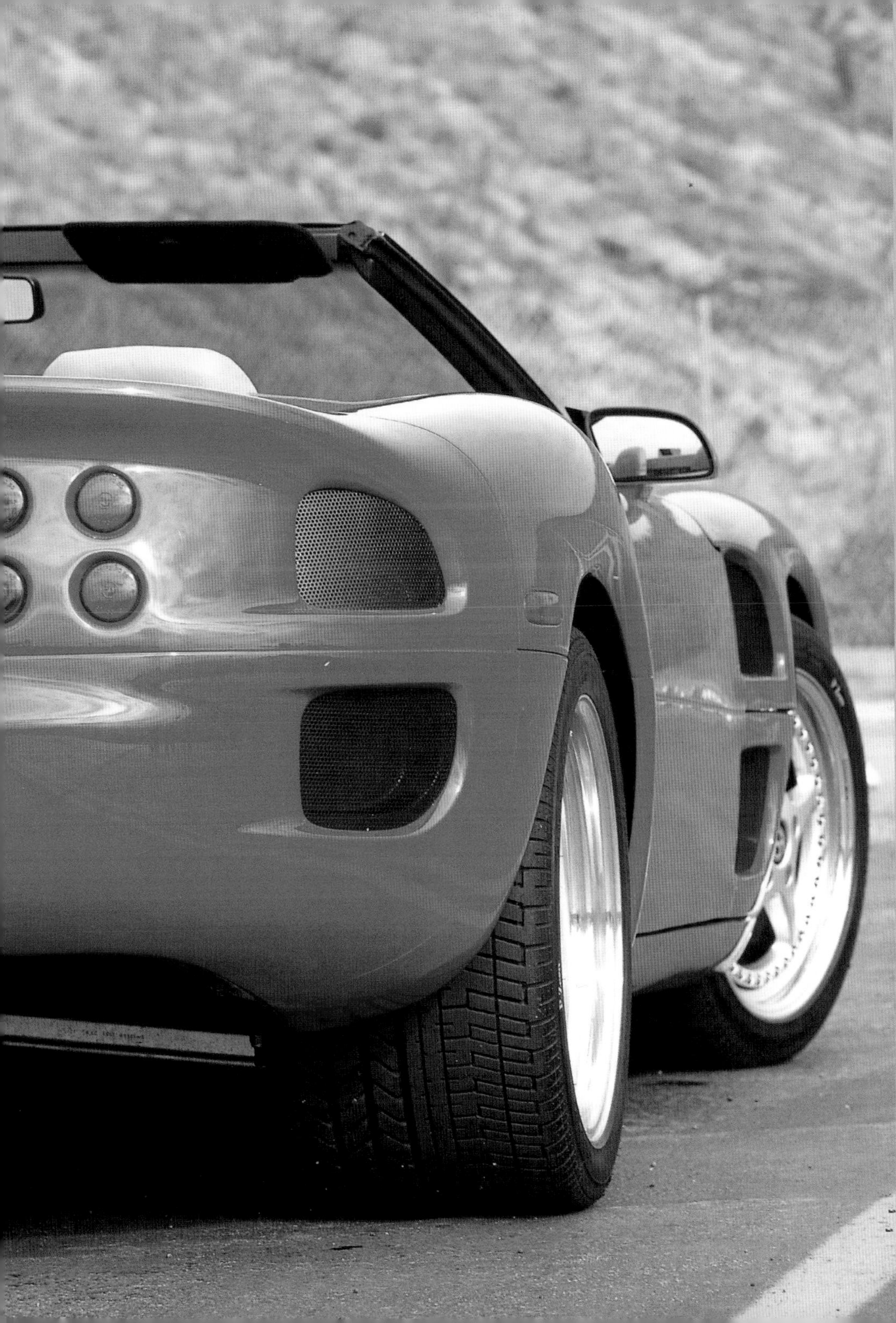

It was born over a coffeepot. Corvette engineer and test driver John Heinricy was talking with Corvette chief engineer Dave Hill over a batch of java about ways to usher out the C4 in style. They figured that if they limited production of a special Corvette to 1,000 units, it would give the outgoing generation some attention, as the public would know that the C5 was just around the corner.

As per the conversation, 1,000 Grand Sports were built—810 coupes and 190

1996 CORVETTE GRAND SPORT

Price: $45,390
Engine: 330-horsepower, 5.7-liter V-8
0–60: 4.9 seconds
Top speed: 168 miles per hour

convertibles. All of them were painted Admiral Blue, with a white stripe and a pair of red hash marks on the front fender to honor the original 1963 Corvette Grand

Sports. Under the paint was a grenade of an engine, the durable LT4. With a 10.8:1 compression ratio, aluminum heads, an aggressive camshaft, and huge valves, the small-block engine made 30 more horsepower than the standard Corvette LT1. The Grand Sport could vault down the local drag strip in just 13.7 seconds, tripping the lights at 105.1 miles per hour.

But with the huge rubber at each fender, the Grand Sport could tackle corners with aplomb. On a skid pad, it would generate 0.88g lateral force. The brakes were no slouch either, bringing the Grand Sport to a stop from 60 miles per hour in just 121 feet. A well-rounded package, the Grand Sport ensured the C4 went out on a high note.

Did You Know?

Two interior color choices were available on the Grand Sport: all black or a red/black combination.

CHAPTER 5
FIFTH GENERATION, 1997-2004

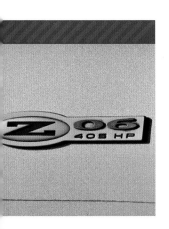

As the 1990s rolled on, it was clear that the automotive landscape was changing, especially regarding sports cars. Traditional builders such as Ferrari and Porsche were flourishing. Acura, long a builder of sedate transportation, had released the NSX, giving every manufacturer fits. Chevrolet was more than a bit worried, as the Corvette was getting long in the tooth, and it increasingly looked like a rolling showroom for yestertech.

So around 1990, the Bowtie crowd started the process of creating a virtually clean-sheet design for the next generation Corvette. It had to be faster, more agile, and better built and still carry on the visual continuity of Corvette heritage. This was no small task, but General Motors is blessed with some of the finest engineers and designers in the business.

In late 1996, the world's motor press traveled to Bowling Green, Kentucky, to see and drive the new C5 Corvette. It was a virtually new car from bumper to bumper, incorporating engineering practices not often seen at General Motors. The steel frame was built around a pair of hydroformed rails, and the crossmembers were welded in place. That process helped increase the C5's structural rigidity considerably.

To the stiff chassis was added an all-aluminum suspension, with the rear suspension being an all-new design for Corvette. For the first time, the transmission was actually a transaxle, combining the trans and differential into one compact unit. This configuration came with a lot of upside for the Corvette: weight distribution was improved, as the transmission's heft in the rear helped balance out the engine's weight. By moving the transmission aft, the interior tunnel could be narrower, opening up the footwells. And with the transaxle in place, the engine could be mounted farther rearward, aiding in weight distribution. The upside of this was the C5's ability to generate a coffee-spilling 0.93g lateral load.

Speaking of the interior, it, too, was an all-new design. Gone were digital displays, replaced by the analog needles preferred by race car drivers. The shifter was a tauter unit than the C4's. All the controls were placed throughout the interior in a much more ergonomic fashion.

But a large part of any Corvette's appeal is its exterior, and the C5, with its flowing lines and wind tunnel–friendly curves, cut the air with a coefficient of drag of 0.29, very slippery indeed. The low drag had a couple of benefits, such as reducing fuel consumption, lowering interior noise at speed, and improving high-speed stability. Make no mistake: this Corvette was capable of go-directly-to-jail speeds. Yet its slate of electronic aids helped a driver get out of

sticky situations that would have had dire results even the generation before. The throttle was now a drive-by-wire control, using computers to maintain the proper fuel/air mixture for maximum performance.

Chevrolet had a lot riding on the C5 Corvette, including the vehicle's continued existence. Some in General Motors saw the Corvette as a waste of resources. Fortunately, cooler heads prevailed, resulting in the most dynamic Corvette yet.

In 1998, the Corvette was tapped to pace the Indianapolis 500-Mile race for the fourth time. As in years prior, Chevrolet pulled out all the stops in creating a visually striking vehicle to lead the pack around the 2.5-mile Brickyard. Cloaked in Radar Blue paint with vibrant graphics and retina-burning yellow wheels, this pace car was almost an affront to the senses. The interior was not ignored either, with a black/yellow leather combo so hot that you could almost feel it through your pants.

1998 CORVETTE PACE CAR REPLICA

Price: $50,029
Engine: 345-horsepower, 5.7-liter, fuel-injected V-8
0-60: 4.9 seconds
Top speed: 172 miles per hour

Like most Corvette pace cars, Chevrolet didn't have to do anything under the hood to keep its sports car at the head of the class. Its standard V-8 delivered plenty of pacing power, and while it's safe to say it was on

the actual pace car, customers could order the new optional Active Handling chassis control system (J4L), which used a raft of sensors to keep the shiny side up and make the driver look like a hero.

Two transmissions were available on the pace cars bound for garages: a 4-speed automatic or the optional extra-cost 6-speed manual. Either one would help this pace car break every speed limit in the land.

The RPO Z4Z Pace Car Package (automatic) fattened the bottom line by $5,039. Chevy built just 1,163 Indy 500 pace car replicas, including 5 pilot C5's that were for factory use only. While the vast majority of them were sold at Chevrolet dealers across the United States, a select number were shipped for sale overseas. By the way, golfer Greg Norman was scheduled to drive the actual pace car, but a shoulder injury kept him out. Parnelli Jones handled the job on race day.

Did You Know?

The winner of the Indy 500 gets a pace car as a gift; in 1998 Eddie Cheever Jr. rolled off into the sunset behind the wheel of his.

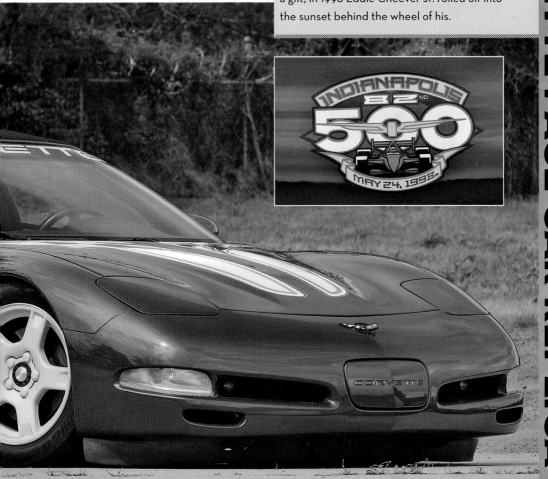

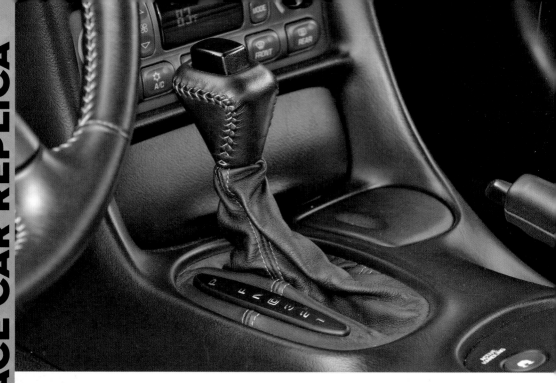

Reeves Callaway claimed that the C5-based Callaway C12 was built "to a standard rather than a price." This would help explain the healthy price of admission. Only 20 of the ground-bound missiles were built, and most went to high-profile customers. The only areas of a stock C5 that were left alone during the C12's manufacturing process were the greenhouse and the roof. Virtually everything, inside and out, was replaced, re-covered, or modified. Each car

1998 CALLAWAY C12

Price: $178,500
Engine: 440-horsepower, 5.7-liter V-8
0–60: 4.3 seconds
Top speed: 189 miles per hour

was tailored to its buyer, from paint to upholstery. Yet the reason the C12 street car was built was to homologate the design to allow the racing version to hit the track.

Being a Callaway, the under-hood situation was explosive. The 440-horse engine was based on the LS1 small-block. The standard camshafts were ditched, replaced with a custom-ground bump stick. Balancing and blueprinting were standard, and the engine computer was recalibrated. Torque grew to 420 lb-ft. That was more than enough to smoke the expensive Pirelli P-Zero tires. The dramatic body was designed by Paul Deutschman and was built using composite materials. Because the C12 wore such wide tires, the width of the car was enlarged 5.1 inches to cover the big meats. This was not a car for the shy.

Did You Know?
So heavily modified were C5s during their conversion into C12s that when C12s were brought into Europe, they were registered as Callaways, not Corvettes.

As the twentieth century wound to an end, Chevrolet's Corvette saw a number of firsts. The most significant was the release of a third model in the Corvette line, the hardtop model. Looking like a Corvette convertible with a hardtop on, it was intended to be a lighter Corvette, with a lower level of standard equipment, and a subsequent lower price. Chevrolet was not very good at hiding the fact that the hardtop model was built for competition. This model was only available with a 6-speed manual transmission and the aggressive Z51 suspension.

1999 CORVETTE COUPE

Price: $39,171
Engine: 345-horsepower, 5.7-liter, fuel-injected V-8
0-60: 3.8 seconds
Top Speed: 171 miles per hour

Yet the most popular model among buyers was the coupe. And in the truest Chevrolet fashion, options could be ladled on. One of the most technologically advanced RPOs was UV6, the Heads Up Instrument Display, a $375 feature that projected basic

information onto the windshield in front of the driver.

Next-generation airbags were introduced on the 1999 Corvette, which meant they opened with less force. On the other side of the coin, more force was delivered via the LS1 5.7-liter V-8. With 345-horsepower on tap, it wasn't hard to get into a position where your driver's license was at risk. In an effort to keep the tires on the straight and narrow, RPO's F45 (Selective Real Time Damping) and JL4 (Active Handling System) were available on the coupe and convertible models. The result was leech-like grip and confidence-inspiring handling. Whichever version of 1999 Corvette was put in the garage, it was a guarantee of vehicle Nirvana.

Did You Know?

Readers of the highly regarded automotive magazine *AutoWeek* voted the Corvette America's best car (July 5, 1999).

Chevrolet long had a policy of making gradual changes over a model's life, and the Corvette hewed to this policy. Midway through the fifth generation, the Corvette convertible was the recipient of subtle improvements for 2000, such as new wheels, shifter modifications, and seat material upgrades. The lock cylinder on the passenger-side door was eliminated,

2000 CORVETTE CONVERTIBLE

Price: $45,900
Engine: 345-horsepower, 5.7-liter V-8
0–60: 4.9 seconds
Top speed: 171 miles per hour

as the door could be remotely unlocked with the keyless entry system. A door lock cylinder remained in the driver-side door to allow for entry in case of a battery failure.

Torch Red, as seen on this example, was one of the most popular colors, with 2,575 ragtops painted this ticket-bait hue. Beneath the paint were body panels made of sheet-molded compound; fiberglass had not been used as the body material for years. Under the hood, the excellent LS1 small-block engine continued to generate thrust. With 350 lb-ft of torque, the 18-inch rear tires were at serious risk. Yet the Corvette convertible was an excellent grand tourer; it could go 425 miles between fill-ups.

Did You Know?
A new color for 2000, Millennium Yellow, cost $500 extra due to the need for a special tinted clear coat.

Three body styles were available in 2000: a hardtop, a convertible, and this popular coupe. A tapering rear window reminiscent of the backlight on the second-generation Corvette hinged up, allowing access to a huge, 25-cubic-foot storage area behind the bucket seats. The 2000 Corvette was a car of refinement, with new forged thin-spoke wheels, an upgraded Z51 "Performance Handling Package," and new paint finishes.

2000 CORVETTE COUPE

Price: $39,475
Engine: 345-horsepower, 5.7-liter V-8
0–60: 4.8 seconds
Top speed: 172 miles per hour

The cost of the optional magnesium wheels dropped from $3,000 to $2,000. The Corvette wore 17-inch wheels in the front

and huge 18-inch rollers in the rear. With 345 horsepower, it was important to get the power to the ground. And with rolling stock this big, handling became legendary.

Of the three body styles available, the coupe was the most popular, with 18,113 sold. RPO CC3, a blue-tinted removable roof panel, cost $650 and was installed on 5,605 Corvettes. It had a UV-ray shield built into the glass, minimizing the sun's ability to heat the interior and give the occupants sunburn. Buyers wanting to pick up their new purchases in an unusual setting could opt for RPO R8C, the National Corvette Museum factory delivery option, a deal at just $490.

Did You Know?

The weight difference between the coupe and the convertible was only 2 pounds; the coupe was the lighter of the two Corvettes.

The fifth-generation Corvette entered its last year of production with the thrilling Z06 in the lineup. Reviving a venerated name in Corvette lore, the Z06 hit showrooms in 2001 and proved to be a popular model, especially among owners who stretched their cars on a racetrack. When the Z06 was introduced in 2001, its LS6 engine developed a hefty 385 horses. By the time this 2004 Z06 rolled out of the Bowling Green plant, it was churning out a lusty

2004 CORVETTE Z06

Price: $52,385
Engine: 405-horsepower, 5.7-liter V-8
0–60: 3.7 seconds
Top speed: 171 miles per hour

405 horsepower, a very respectable number for a normally aspirated engine.

The Z06 was full of race-bred parts, with a heavy emphasis on handling prowess.

Chevrolet made every effort to reduce the Z06's weight, such as installing a titanium exhaust system and a bigger front stabilizer bar and increasing the rear transverse composite leaf springs' bending resistance. The Z06 was available in only the hardtop model.

The LS6 engine, while based on the LS1, generated about 12 percent more power. Some of the paths to power were an increased compression ratio, new pistons,

enlarged fuel injectors, and a high-lift camshaft. The redline of this potent engine was 6,500 rpm, and under the whip it would swing the tachometer needle clockwise in a blur. This was a race car you could live with every day. Sounds like a win-win!

Did You Know?

For 2004, Chevrolet released a commemorative Z06. It used a carbon fiber hood for the first time in Corvette history, shaving 10.6 pounds off the curb weight.

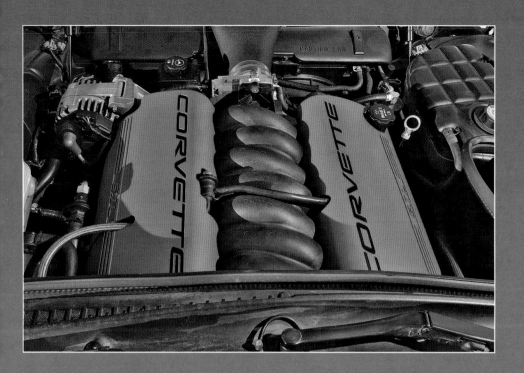

2004 CORVETTE Z06

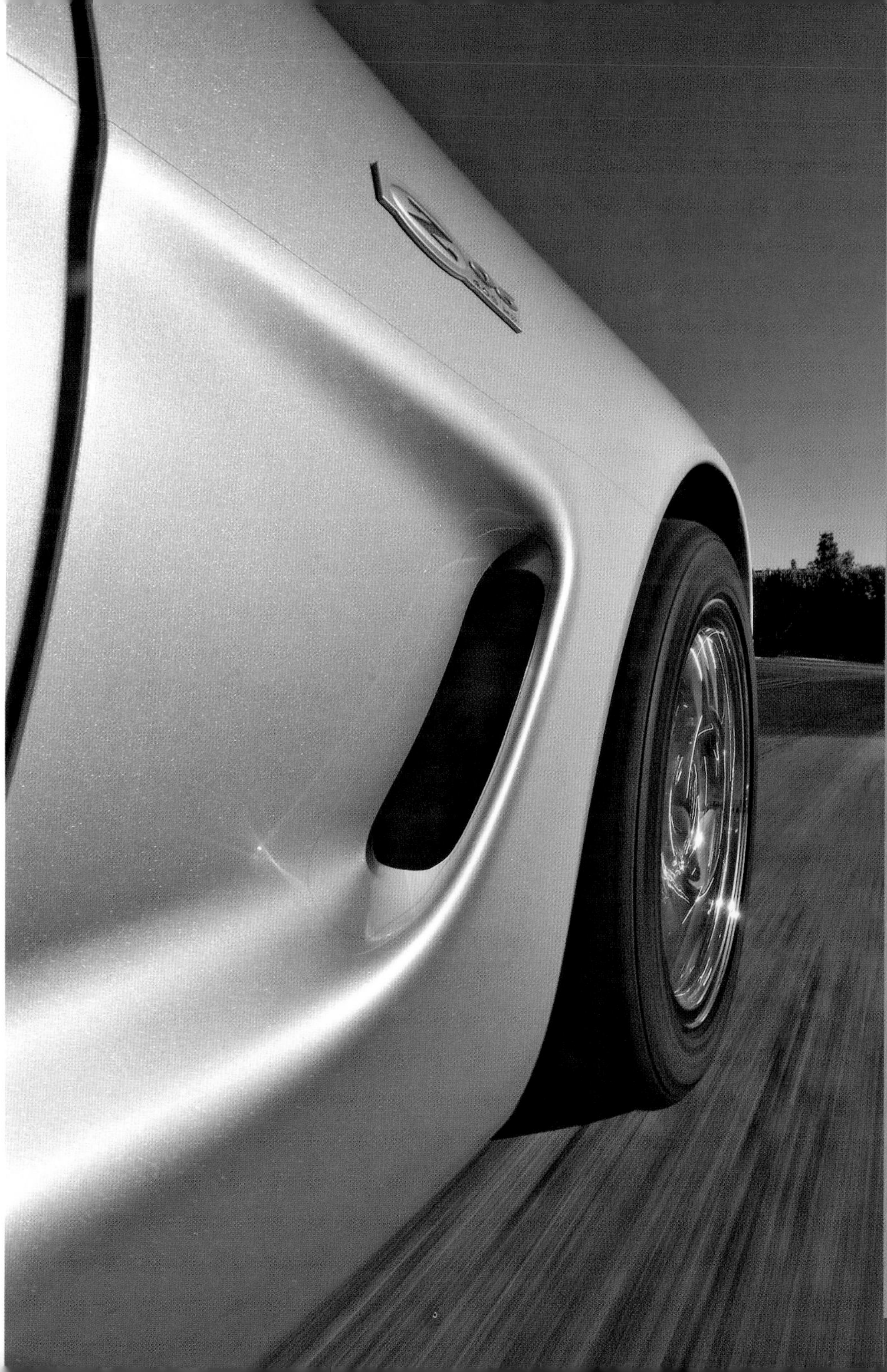

CHAPTER 6
SIXTH GENERATION, 2005-PRESENT

To paraphrase a Midwestern chemical company, the Corvette embraced "better living through computers." Based on lessons learned in competition and demands from customers, the 2005 Corvette ushered in new levels of comfort, performance, and quality. The sixth-generation Corvette was easy to differentiate from the prior model: the newest Corvette wore crisper lines, was shorter and narrower, and, for the first time since 1962, had exposed headlights. But most of the changes weren't visible to the eye.

At first glance, the sixth-generation Corvette had a slightly different body, but the changes started with the chassis. This component was heavily modified from the fifth-gen model, including a lengthening of the wheelbase by 1.2 inches to 105.7 inches. This change allowed engineers to maintain the amount of interior room in the car while exterior dimensions shrank. The overall length of the car was shortened by 5.1 inches, and the car's width was reduced by 1.1 inches.

Technology was being fed into the Corvette in shovelfuls, and the result was improved power, reduced emissions, increased entertainment, and better handling. In 2006, a historic name in Corvette lore returned. It was the Z06, brimming with big power and superb handling. Electronics helped its 427-cubic-inch engine deliver horsepower at a level that demanded respect, yet it could shuffle around town in a docile fashion when needed.

Refinement and special editions were the order of the day for 2007, as the Ron Fellows Z06 Special Edition and the Indy 500 Edition vied along with the burnished standard Corvette for buyers' attention. Bigger brakes helped rein in the velocity that the Corvette gathered so easily. Stereo controls were improved, and more interior options were offered.

Model year 2008 saw a bigger base engine with more power—an area that some thought didn't need enlargement. Fresh levels of horsepower continued to be extracted from the Chevrolet small-block engine, much to customers' delight. Once again, the Corvette led the field at the Indianapolis 500, and the public was offered two graphic and paint schemes to commemorate the event.

Just when Corvette enthusiasts thought they had seen everything that Corvette could offer, the brutal 2009 ZR1 arrived (no hyphen this time). With its scary power, aggressive looks, and blinding speed, it was no surprise that high-performance driving school was included with the purchase. In addition, Corvettes across the entire '09 line enjoyed upgrades, ranging from increased lubrication to traction control.

The Corvette menu grew in 2010 to include the return of an old friend, the Grand Sport. Slipping into the niche above the base car, and below the Z06, it paid tribute to former Corvette glories while returning a best-of-both-worlds experience. Corvette had a model for everyone, from daily commuter to track terror.

For 2011, there were more Corvette models available than ever before. Between the base model, coupe, and convertible, Grand Sport, Z06, and ZR1, the choices were staggering. And new for 2011 was a program that allowed the buyer of either a Z06 or a ZR1 to enter the engine assembly plant and help build the powerplant for his or her car under the tutelage of a factory engine builder. It was just another level of Corvette passion. The sixth-generation Corvette really is the best one—yet!

As good as a stock Corvette is, there's always an element who feels that more is, well, more. Lingenfelter Performance Engineering has a long history of coaxing stupid power from Corvettes, and this Velocity Yellow example is typical of the kind of ticket bait the firm sells.

Under the hood is a Lingenfelter M112 supercharger kit, as well as a Comp Cams

2006 LINGENFELTER CORVETTE

Price: $134,000
Engine: 640-horsepower, 6.0-liter V-8
0–60: 4.1 seconds
Top speed: 192 miles per hour

camshaft and a set of Dynatech headers. At the end of the exhaust system is a set of Magnaflow Magnapack mufflers, with a snarl that begs for a street fight. The result is an LS2 engine that's cranking out more than 600 horsepower. On the street, on pump gas.

Being able to stop is as important as feeding power to the rear tires, and this Lingenfelter Corvette was fitted with a set of Z51-spec binders from StopTech. Slam on the brake pedal at speed, and you'd better have your seat belt on.

Did You Know?

John Lingenfelter built the engine in the record-breaking Callaway Sledgehammer Corvette.

Want to drive a race car on the street? Here's how you do it: contact famed race car maker Pratt & Miller, hand them your Z06 and a big check, and you'll get have the baddest Corvette on the block. Probably in your city too.

With a Katech Performance–built 8.2-liter all-aluminum Dart small-block under the carbon fiber hood and with 11.1 compression, you'll swear you're on pregrid every time you fire it up. A bespoke Corsa stainless-steel exhaust system emits a threatening growl at idle, turning into a roar when the engine gathers revs.

But this car, owned by Jay Leno, is also a showcase for responsible performance, as the engine runs on E85 ethanol fuel. Pratt & Miller, builders of the famed C6.R race cars, worked their magic on this vehicle, such as fitting carbon fiber front body panels sourced

from the C6R program, a 1.6-inch-wider body to accommodate the huge rubber, and a custom interior. No exposed parts inside; it's all supple leather and high-tech materials.

A near–race car needs quality rolling stock, and with BBS center-lock alloy wheels surrounded by Michelin tires, the C6RS sticks to the ground like a hungry leech. Ideal for near-race experiences.

2007 CORVETTE C6RS

Price: $178,500 plus donor car
Engine: 600-horsepower, 8.2-liter V-8
0–60: 3.7 seconds
Top speed: 192 miles per hour

Did You Know?

Pratt & Miller offers C6RSs that run on regular gasoline and develop 760 horsepower. Bring money.

The sixth-generation Corvette is a stunning piece of engineering right out of the box. But there's always a market for customers wanting to own the big dog. This is a very big dog. Does your daily drive top out at 207 miles per hour? Neither does mine. But Callaway has engineered and styled a C6-based race car for the road. Chock-full of bespoke go-fast bits, it looks as though it belongs on a starting grid rather than at the grocery store. Actually, it's at home in both locales.

2007 CALLAWAY C16
Price: $173,000
Engine: 650-horsepower, 6.2-liter V-8
0–60: 3.3 seconds
Top speed: 207 miles per hour

Under the skin, most of the mechanical components have either been upgraded or flat-out replaced. From its coil-over suspension with double adjustable

aluminum dampers with external reservoirs and special Callaway front and rear tubular stabilizer bars to the Callaway Le Mans GT six-piston (front) and four-piston (rear) brake calipers, optional carbon ceramic pads and rotors, and huge Michelin PS2 ZP tires (285/30ZR19 front; 335/25ZR20 rear), this machine oozes business.

The interior wasn't ignored either. Optional packages allowed a buyer to trim out the cockpit in any color and material known. And for just an additional $68,800, the engine output could be raised to 700 horses. A set of custom Schedoni luggage was a mere $8,800. The C16 could haul more than . . . well, you know.

Did You Know?
Callaway has a long history competing in the Le Mans 24-hour race. Competition really improves the breed.

CALLAWAY
POWERFULLY ENGINEERED AUTOMOBILES™

More. That's what the Corvette offered for 2008. An increase in engine displacement, from 6.0 liters to 6.2, gave the Chevrolet a bit more beans. The engine was sufficiently changed to warrant a new engine model designation, LS3. With an aluminum block utilizing cast-iron cylinder liners, the engine was an excellent blend of low weight and durability. An optional dual-mode 2.5-inch exhaust system used throttle position and engine speed to open a set of vacuum-operated valves, reducing back pressure,

2008 CORVETTE CONVERTIBLE

Price: $54,335
Engine: 430-horsepower, 6.2-liter V-8
0-60: 4.3 seconds
Top speed: 190 miles per hour

increasing the exhaust notes' volume, and giving the engine an additional six horsepower. The cylinder heads were styled after the LS7 units, the valves

were enlarged, and the high-flow fuel injectors were "borrowed" from the 505-horsepower Z06's LS7 engine. The engine beauty covers utilized sound-deadening material to reduce valvetrain noise. Sometimes technology is pretty neat.

Other upgrades for 2008 included improvements to the manual transmission's shift effort; faster shift times on paddle-shift-equipped cars, improving the rack-and-pinion-steering feel; and a reworked interior with upgraded materials. The optional Magnetic Selective Ride Control, RPO F55, cost $1,995 and was worth every penny. A driver could, at the twist of a knob, transform the Corvette from smooth cruiser to brutal racer. Like I said, technology can be pretty neat.

Did You Know?

Once again in 2008, the Corvette was the Indy 500 pace car, with Emerson Fittipaldi handling driving duties. A Z06 model running on E85 ethanol fuel was used.

While the ZR1 returned to the Corvette camp in 2009, the vast majority of buyers brought home the base Corvette, which, when you factor in the incredible capability versus the price, was one of the best performance buys anywhere. Under the skin, the 2009 base model was pretty much a carryover model, with most of the attention from Chevrolet being lavished on the new-for-2009 ZR1 model. But that's not

2009 CORVETTE COUPE

Price: $47,895
Engine: 430-horsepower, 6.2-liter V-8
0–60: 4.1 seconds
Top speed: 189 miles per hour

exactly a bad thing; the 430-horse base-level Corvette was one hell of a performance bargain. The base Corvette cost less than half what the ZR1 cost. Easier to insure too.

New for 2009 was a new Bosch ABS, traction control, and an active handling system. The steering shaft was changed from an aluminum part to steel, increasing the feel of the variable-ratio power steering. For the first time, Bluetooth connectivity was offered in a Corvette.

The build quantity for 2009 Corvettes was spread out among the various models; 8,737 base coupes were built, while 3,343 base convertibles were sold. Up the Corvette ladder, Chevrolet assembled 3,461 Z06s and 1,415 of the ground-shaking ZR1s. Total production was 16,956 units.

Did You Know?
Hertz offered Corvettes in its rental fleet in 2008, and the company bought more Corvettes in 2009.

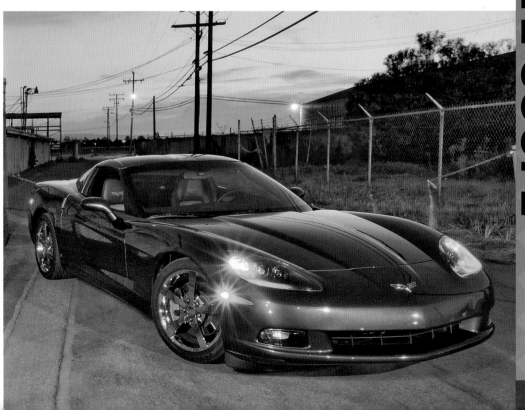

As if a Corvette buyer doesn't have enough to choose from these days, in 2010 Chevrolet brought back a name rich in automotive history, the Grand Sport. Blending bits of various Corvette packages into a superbly balanced vehicle, the Grand Sport started with a base coupe or convertible, then added wider bodywork and tires; an upgraded suspension; a Z06 splitter, rear spoiler, and brakes; a dry-sump lubrication system in manual-transmission-equipped coupes; and more. A pair of front fender slashes made it

2010 GRAND SPORT

Price: $55,720 (coupe)
Engine: 430-horsepower, 6.0-liter V-8
0–60: 4.0 seconds
Top speed: 190 miles per hour

clear that this Corvette was not your normal Chevrolet sports car. The Grand Sport package replaced the Z51 option.

Under the one-piece clamshell hood lived an LS3, displacing 6.0 liters and rated

at a healthy 430 horsepower. Yet with the gearing that Chevrolet gave the Grand Sport, it was possible to get nearly 30 miles per gallon on the highway. The problem, as with all Corvettes, was keeping your foot out of it. Manual-transmission-equipped Corvettes even came with launch control to further the risk to one's driver's license.

It was a value-rich opportunity to have your Corvette cake and eat it too. The Grand Sport was able to acquit itself well on weekend track day sessions, yet it didn't abuse a driver slogging along on a morning commute. It was a popular model as well, with the coupe version outselling all other Corvette models for 2010, with 3,707 going to good garages.

Did You Know?

The wheels on the Grand Sport came with a standard silver-painted finish, but they could be ordered with an optional competition gray finish or in chrome.

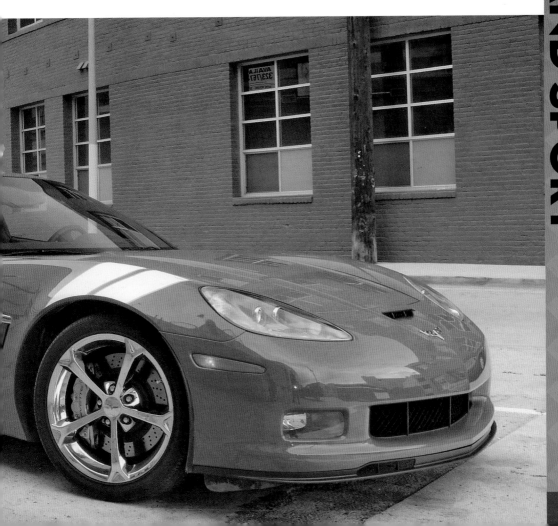

Power to weight. It's a formula as old as automobile racing. The 2011 Z06 is a rolling tribute to the spectacle of power over weight. It has a 7.0-liter normally aspirated V-8 that will crank out 505 horsepower all day long without breaking a sweat. The engine uses a dry-sump oiling system to prevent lubrication starvation under sustained high-g maneuvers. The six-speed manual transmission is connected to a limited-slip differential, feeding power into tires big enough to feel at home on a Le Mans race

car. A heads-up display tells drivers how far over the speed limit they're going. And all of this is in a dealer's showroom. Is this a great country or what?

2011 CORVETTE ZO6

Price: $82,725
Engine: 505-horsepower, 7.0-liter V-8
0–60: 3.7 seconds
Top speed: 198 miles per hour

Unlike the base and Grand Sport model Corvettes, which use a steel frame, the race-bred Z06 sits on an aluminum frame. Onto that is bolted no small number of components that would be right at home under a pure race car, including coolers for the oil, transmission, and differential; an all-aluminum SLA suspension; six-piston front and four-piston rear cross-drilled brakes; and the incredible LS7 engine.

For buyers wanting an even more intense Z06 experience, Chevrolet released the Z06 Carbon Limited Edition, with a build quantity of 500 units. It's a tribute to the 50th anniversary of the Corvette racing at Le Mans.

Did You Know?

The dual-mode exhaust system breathes through 4-inch tips and, when open, lets everyone within a mile know that the engine is working—hard.

There are big dogs, and then there are really big dogs. This is as big as they get. Packed with the most powerful engine that General Motors has ever put into a production car, the newest ZR1 is a technological showcase for the Corvette. With a supercharged LS9 6.2-liter under the polycarbonate window in the center of the hood, the ZR1 uses a nearly race car engine to develop a staggering amount of power, yet it can be

2011 CORVETTE ZR1

Price: $125,195
Engine: 638-horsepower, 6.2-liter V-8
0–60: 3.5 seconds
Top speed: 205 miles per hour

driven daily. Let's just hope that your daily drive includes some loooong stretches of open road.

Going fast in a straight line is one thing, but roads, and racetracks, have curves. The ZR1 is designed to cling to the tarmac like a politician to a dollar. When it comes time to bring the ZR1 to a halt, its cross-drilled Brembo ceramic brakes shrug off repeated applications from high speed.

Virtually every feature possible to cram into a Corvette is in the ZR1, including Magnetic Selective Ride Control, active handling, a traction control system, and speed-sensitive variable-ration rack-and-pinion power steering. It adds up to the greatest Corvette Chevrolet has built so far. It will embarrass exotics costing twice as much yet deliver fuel economy on the highway in the 20-miles-per-gallon range. It's the best of all worlds!

Did You Know?

On the drag strip, the Corvette ZR1 covers a quarter mile in just 11.5 seconds at 126.9 miles per hour. It needs only 7.6 seconds to reach 100 miles per hour.

It's not an accident that one of the crossed flags on the nose of every Corvette is checkered. Since the mid-1950s, Corvettes have competed, and won, in virtually every kind of automobile race around the world. From weekend gymkhanas in a high school parking lot to the 24 Hours of Le Mans, Corvettes have been able competitors.

The current generation of Corvettes has been carrying on the tradition. Working with Pratt & Miller, the C6.R continues the momentum of the C5-R program, with numerous wins in the American Le Mans Series (ALMS), the FIA GT Championship, the aforementioned 24 Hours of Le Mans, and SCCA races.

Katech builds the C6.R's 7.0-liter engine, closely based on the LS7 found in the Z06. Known as the LS7.R, this powerplant won the Global Motorsport Engine of the Year award in 2006.

Pratt & Miller worked with General Motors to develop the race car concurrently with the production car, resulting in the

ability to tailor the street car to race needs with minimal trouble. Air conditioning is one example. Race cars tend to cook the driver; with A/C, the driver stays cool and can focus longer, critical in endurance racing. Many details that went onto the race car eventually found their way onto the street version. Splitters, air dams, spoilers, and ducting were all proven in the crucible of competition before making it to the showroom. Racing really does improve the breed.

CORVETTE C6.R

Price: A whole lot
Engine: 590-horsepower, 7.0-liter V-8
0–60: 2.6 seconds
Top speed: 196 miles per hour

Did You Know?

The Corvette C6.R debuted in 2005 and has been a highly competitive race car. It won its class at the 12 Hours of Sebring four straight years: 2006, 2007, 2008, and 2009!

Chevrolet has never been one to let an anniversary pass without a suitable amount of fanfare, both in advertising and on the cars. The Corvette is the oldest current vehicle for sale in America, and when the Bow Tie's 100th birthday rolled around in 2011, there was a celebratory edition ready to start the party. The Centennial Edition, RPO 4LT, is a special paint and suspension package, and it's a striking option. The paint is a rich dark grey metallic, and it's complimented by satin-black graphics and unique Centennial satin-black wheels and

2012 CORVETTE GRAND SPORT CENTENNIAL EDITION

Price: $72,070
Engine: 436-horsepower, 6.2-liter fuel-injected V-8
0-60: 3.9 seconds
Top speed: 192 mph

red brake calipers. As an onlooker said to me while I was photographing this vehicle, "It just looks mean!"

The wow-factor doesn't stop on the body; every Centennial Edition came standard

with GM's Magnetic Selective Ride Control. This feature is one of those must-haves on a Corvette. It can transform Chevy's sports car from a comfortable touring vehicle to a track-ready beast at the twist of a knob. It's worth every penny.

The interior, long a source of complaints among the Corvette faithful, received a long overdue upgrade. Ebony leather with contrasting red stitching on the seats, steering wheel, console, and shifter, all touch points, presented an upscale feel. The seats, source of many lower back pains, were improved.

The base sticker price of all this Corvette goodness was $72,070. Buyers could ladle even more options on as desired, but for the money, nothing could come close. The Centennial Edition package was available on all Corvettes, including the Z06 and ZR1.

Did You Know?
Chevrolet used an image of Louis Chevrolet in racing garb on the Centennial Edition's B-pillar, wheel center caps, and steering wheel hub.

INDEX